ONE MIND MANY THOUGHTS

Born and educated in Delhi, **Pravesh Jain** is a quiet philanthropist. His Paras Foundation runs an old-age home, a school for 180 street children and an institution for the visually impaired, all in Delhi. He is also a successful businessman. Columns written by Pravesh appear regularly in The *Pioneer* and *The Asian Age*. This debutant author is well into writing two more books—both fiction.

ONE MIND MANY THOUGHTS

NOTES FROM A COMMON MAN'S DIARY

PRAVESH JAIN

Published by
Rupa Publications India Pvt. Ltd 2014
7/16, Ansari Road, Daryaganj
New Delhi 110002

Sales centres:
Allahabad Bengaluru Chennai
Hyderabad Jaipur Kathmandu
Kolkata Mumbai

Copyright © Pravesh Jain 2014

The views and opinions expressed in this book are the author's own and the facts are as reported by him which have been verified to the extent possible, and the publishers are not in any way liable for the same.

All rights reserved.
No part of this publication may be reproduced, transmitted, or stored in a retrieval system, in any form or by any means, electronic, mechanical, photocopying, recording or otherwise, without the prior permission of the publisher.

ISBN: 978-81-291-2465-4

First impression 2014

10 9 8 7 6 5 4 3 2 1

The moral right of the author has been asserted.

Printed at Replika Press Pvt. Ltd., India

This book is sold subject to the condition that it shall not, by way of trade or otherwise, be lent, resold, hired out, or otherwise circulated, without the publisher's prior consent, in any form of binding or cover other than that in which it is published.

To my father, late D.C. Jain
and
my mother, Sushila Jain

Contents

Foreword   *xi*
Introduction   *xv*

Part 1

1. A Darkness at Noon — 3
2. What's your Nexus? — 8
3. A Child's Cry — 14
4. The Second Freedom Struggle — 18
5. Speak-Up to Ease-Up — 23
6. More Power to Woman Power — 26
7. Euthanasia: A Blessing or a Curse? — 29
8. A Mission Before Us — 32
9. Let Creativity Be! — 34
10. Three Monkeys are Still Around! — 37
11. To the Awakened India — 40
12. No Space for the Poor Here! — 42
13. A Travesty of Democracy — 46
14. Disabled or Differently Abled? — 49
15. Stop Killing the Girl Child! — 53
16. Widows: Victims of Age Old Traditions — 56
17. The Two Lives of a Politician — 60
18. Are We a Nation of Fictitious Values and Double Standards? — 63
19. We Want Justice! — 68

Part 2

1. Confessions of a Romantic — 75
2. Change with Continuity — 78
3. Traditional Indian Gestures and their Inherent Godliness — 80
4. The Son of God as the Sun God — 84
5. To Love or Not to Love — 86
6. Love Thy Servants — 89
7. An Ode to a Mother — 92
8. The Everlasting Beauty of Sibling Bonds — 94
9. Woh To Apke Baap Ke Bhi Baap Hai — 96
10. Your Wife, your Life — 98
11. Long Live the Father! — 100
12. A Wedding to Remember — 102
13. Friendship is Forever — 105
14. Know Thy Neighbour! — 108
15. Different Shades of Love — 111

Part 3

1. Be Positive — 117
2. One Pledge at a Time — 121
3. Pop the Happiness Pill — 123
4. Blame the Blame-Game — 125
5. Prayer for Peace — 128
6. Mother Teresa: An Inspiration for Generations — 130
7. Positive is What Positive Does — 132
8. Thought for Food — 136
9. The Golden Rule of Humility — 140
10. Have Will to Succeed — 142
11. Peace within is Life's Best Attainment — 145
12. Lessons in Anger Management — 148

13. Do Good to Feel Good	150
14. Follow the Heart's Path to Invention	152
15. Spiritual Dhongis	155
16. A Licence to Kill	158
17. Marriage of Souls or Status?	161
18. My Nature, My Mother	165
19. Nature and its Pleasures	168
20. A Cornucopia for All	171
Epilogue	173
Acknowledgements	174

Foreword

Thoughts are a dynamic force. This is what makes all random thoughts very generative and spontaneous. They are also rare and meaningful because they lie beyond any academic discipline. They are, in fact, the products of a fertile and imaginative mind. And, when these thoughts are altruistic and creative, they have a vitality about them; they are revolutionary in character and expand you both mentally and spiritually.

One Mind, Many Thoughts: Notes from a Common Man's Diary is a collection of sensitive and meditative pieces that have their provenance in the author's humanitarian outlook on the one hand, and in his indignation at the total failure of the social, institutional and governmental systems, on the other. The author is also a bit disturbed and anguished by the exploitation of the vulnerable. The measures they shamelessly use, and without any pangs of conscience, against the weak and the helpless.

The author's concern about the sufferings of the people is not written from some ivory tower. He is a major planner and participant in the setting up of a trust—Paras Foundation. This social institution's motto is very transparent: Help all those who are not helped by anyone. In carrying out its humanitarian activities, Paras Foundation does not take any help from the government or any other institution. The Foundation runs an old age home, a school for street children and an institution for the visually impaired, all in Delhi.

Over the years, while implementing the Foundation's various schemes, the author has experienced first-hand the plight, misery and sufferings of people without resources. He himself has seen how the dignity of the poor is often hurt by the resourceful. He is aware of the apathy such people and the government show towards those who have fallen into dire straits. The author has pointed the contrast out very impressively: 'Anyone who has some sense and emotions will be shocked to see what is happening in the name of healthcare in these high end private hospitals. These are not just hospitals with caring doctors around, as you and I expect. These are the healthcare malls with doctors acting as sales officers or marketing managers and the patients as consumers.'

Throughout the book, the author has cogently and sympathetically tried to bring out the vulgar contrast between the poor and the affluent.

What makes this book worth reading is its wide-ranging content. It is a collection of ideas that have been expressed, off and on, on various subjects.

Before you is a creation, which I am sure will interest all serious readers. The author has very skilfully maintained his objectivity too. Yes, he is an angry crusader against injustice and exploitation of any kind! Yet, he is not just a destroyer of the system. He suggests ways to overcome the negativities in life and the system. The book has many facets to offer a searcher. It contains his ruminations on exploitation, corruption, terrorism, bad governance, squandering resources and above all, the growing divide between the rich and the poor.

In this imaginative work, you will find a subtle fusion of the microscopic observation of a pragmatic person with the absolutely transparent utterances of one who genuinely believes in the power of social justice and rejects altogether the hedonistic attitude that transforms a person into a thick-skinned self-seeker.

However, this work also has a philosophical dimension. The author writes about those people who have devoted themselves wholly to the service of mankind and whose creations have made the life of others more comfortable on this planet. He writes about those who face the challenges of life with the spirit of a warrior and who through sheer determination will tackle the obstacles along the way. His observations on personal relationships within a family and in society will serve as an example to many.

I hope that readers will be able to find a solution to some of their problems. One thing is certain, a search through this book will enrich people's minds and hearts, make them aware of the failures of society at large as well as inspire them to contribute their own ideas towards making the world an ideal place to live in.

V.K. Joshi
Author and professor of English

Introduction

When I look back upon my life and the knowledge that I have accumulated over the years, courtesy my own experiences and those of other like-minded people, I realized that my thoughts and ideas could be of some benefit to a larger audience.

And so here is this book!

There are books and then there are books, but there are very few which connect straight with your heart and strike the right chord. In *One Mind, Many Thoughts: Notes from a Common Man's Diary* you have before you not just a book, but a vision of my idea of an India of the future. India, I know, is a land of extremes. One one hand, it is progressing to match the steps of the world's biggest economies, while on the other, it still has a sizeable number of the population living below the poverty line. While young India is full of zest and enthusiasm, it lacks the sustainability to easily make it to the Fortune 500 club. Through this book I have painted this very picture of the changing and already changed India. The book is mainly targeted at the youth, the mainstay of our country, and carries some suggestions on how they can be not just a part of the change, but be the change themselves.

In all earnest, the book is a compilation of random thoughts and at no point does it intend to be preachy. It is not a commentary on the nation, but my understanding of the transformation it has gone through over the years. As we stand on the cusp of another socioeconomic change, I recommend that you read this book as it will take you back in time as well as forward to the future and help you familiarize yourself with the small things which we tend to overlook in life.

I would also like to add that I don't consider myself to be a reformer or a crusader against the malpractices prevalent in society today, but I do believe in the powers of justice and freedom. It is also my conviction that only a vibrant and creative society can stand above malign forces by the virtue of its inherent splendour. Some of the facts and thoughts shared in the book have several sources, including the Internet and books written by eminent people. It just strengthens the fact that there are many others who share my sentiments and are working towards bringing a change to the current scenario.

I will consider that my mission is accomplished if these articles strike a chord with the youth of today and that they inspire and motivate them to be a responsible citizens.

This book will offer you many suggestions and recommendations on myriads of topics, ranging from how to respect the elderly, deal with both love and anger, handle relationships and break-ups, building careers, being a good neighbour and a compassionate employer, living with nature and much more.

While reading the book, some pieces may excite and intrigue you, some may be mysterious or magical, but one thing is certain that you have been offered a variety of thoughts and impressions that will surely help you to change your life for the better and make you happier.

Read on...for who knows you may just find something new, meant exclusively for you!

Part 1

A Darkness at Noon

As the sun sets, a new reality dawns upon me—the reality of today! My mind is filled with thoughts and ideas about my country. One question that worries me most is: Where exactly is my country headed? We are all proud of the achievements we have made and the milestones we have crossed since independence. At the same time we are full of rage and anger at our helpless at the all-pervading corruption, bribery, nepotism, communal divide, class and caste barriers that cloud our future.

Standing knee-deep in the endless waters of the Arabian Sea along Marine Drive in Mumbai, I wonder if I have given back to my nation and her impoverished population as much I have taken from them? Can I really call myself a responsible citizen when, like everyone else, I have knowingly, or unknowingly, contributed to the same evils? For long, a deep wound has been festering within me, day and night. It looks as if life has lost its meaning. Even when surrounded by people, I am haunted by despair.

Our nation today has become like a banana republic. It looks as if democracy is just a euphemism that we use to describe the sorry state of affairs. Gone are the days when democracy meant 'Of the people, for the people, by the people'. In today's parlance it means 'Of the politician and people with power and money, by them and for them'. Those who have the money and means have the right to run the country and live here, however they wish, even though half the population cannot afford one square meal a day. Bureaucrats, white-collar officials and politicians continue to loot the country and stash their accumulated black money in their Swiss bank and benami accounts, while the common man bears the brunt.

Millions die of hunger, malnutrition, lack of medical aid or in natural calamities, and yet, there is no one to help them in the hour of their need. Poor children beg on the streets when they should be studying in school, but who is there to speak on their behalf and help them with their basic needs. NGOs and social workers, too, are busy lobbying with bureaucrats and politicians who have granted them favours. As a result they have lost track of their goals, and fighting for the poor and destitute has taken a backseat, while personal agendas have taken precedence.

Such is the state of our country today. Even the judiciary and judicial system have not remained untouched by the politics of 'you scratch my back and I'll scratch yours'. Judges and lawyers often take favours from politicians and in turn, they help politicians escape from the larger cesspool of corruption and scams. Cases linger on for years, and by the time a judgment is reached, most of the corrupt politicians, bureaucrats, fixers and businessmen are either dead or nothing can be proved against them. I often visit the lower and high courts and have found that small lawyers have become fixers, prominent advocates have amassed huge wealth and have the support of powerful politicians and corporate honchos, and generally behave like the pre-independent British. Millions of cases are pending in various courts. Thousands languish in jail for long periods of time, but who bothers?

The country's political system that has been exploiting our framework for so long needs serious overhauling. For years, our so-called leaders have looted and duped the nation and her citizens for their own selfish needs. Evading taxes, pouring money into illegal businesses through the hawala route, running ghost corporate empires, taking cuts in international deals, being party to scams worth thousands of crores and robbing the poor has become the norm today. Politicians take their power for granted and are openly involved in scam after scam without any fear of public shame or getting caught. What is it that drives them to such levels of greed? Is it money or the lust for power? They are the same people who pledge to work selflessly and honestly for the good of the nation during elections, but when they become ministers their priorities change. When the country's moral and social brigade loses its integrity, who can we look up to? Sadly, there are no role models left.

Unfortunately, people who are selfish and corrupt will go to any length to achieve what they want. For them, power means accumulating as much wealth as they can and grooming their children to be heirs to their thrones. Do only the children of politicians, industrialists and bureaucrats have the right to enjoy a privileged life because of their lineage? Do we have to accept the fact that just because they are someone's son or daughter they can, without any struggle, take the beacon of power forward? Does this mean that the common man has no right to move up the ladder through hard work, zeal, a sense of responsibility and aptitude and shape the future of the country and her people? My heart aches whenever I try to confront such realities.

Some academics and economists see the rising Sensex as a panacea for all the ills we face today. But this seems to be a deliberately misguiding evaluation. The main issue is that who are the people who control the rise and fall of the Sensex? The harsh reality, however, is that even if the Sensex crosses the 40,000 mark, it will not improve the life of the common man. Will the average Indian get nutritious food, good education and proper healthcare? Will it ensure that thousands of farmers do not commit suicide? The answer is a big 'NO', because the stock market and Sensex is a 'financial casino' where a few gain huge amounts, others lose their entire savings and the majority are unaware of it. The stock market is unconcerned with the health of the country, but 'if Obama smiles' it goes up, and 'if Obama sneezes', it goes down.

Corruption is everywhere—among politicians, the bureaucracy, the police and, some would say, even the judiciary. Industrialists just want to expand their empires at the cost of the environment or the poor farmers' lands. Healthcare systems are crumbling; authorities have overlooked the needs of young children like nutritious food and a good education. The poor are getting poorer while the rich get richer.

The government is preoccupied with charting policies and schemes without caring about their consequences on the general public and if they reach those who truly deserve them. The poor are dying inside or outside hospitals and medical institutes because of lack of attention or proper medical aid. Just what is happening around me? Is this the India that visionaries like Mahatma Gandhi, Jawaharlal Nehru, Bhagat Singh, Lal Bahadur Shastri and others had envisioned? Surely they must be turning in their graves at the sorry state the country has been reduced to. The freedom they struggled so hard to achieve has given way to bondage of a different kind. Even though we are a free independent nation, we are getting increasingly entangled in a web of all that is bad and evil.

One Anna is not enough. We need thousands like him. What we need today is a brigade of honest, steadfast people who are ready to sacrifice materialistic pleasures and fight spiritedly against the evils that taint our society. A mere protest or march is not enough. We need a collective movement where each individual is committed to fight against the demons that have corroded our systems. This may sound like wishful thinking as it will take years before such a scenario takes shape. But every effort counts.

Is there an immediate solution to this sad and sorry state of affairs? Till the time that the country's top brass listen to their conscience and accept their faults, nothing will change. The poor will keep dying and the rich will continue to enjoy their wealth for generations. As such thoughts overwhelm me, I think that can ending my life offer solace or put an end to my misery? But then there is always a glimmer of hope that pulls me back when I think of the young Indians who can truly bring about change. It is up to them to keep our hopes alive and to bring about the transformations we all aspire for.

What's your Nexus?

In a country where only connections to higher-ups matter, original ideas and noble intentions lose their relevance and significance. Today, this nation is facing a crisis of identity. It seems as if we only recognize those who are part of some nexus or are the kingpins.

There are times when I feel that there is no place for an honest, noble and sincere person in this country. Is this the independent India of our dreams? What is happening all around? Is this really a country worth living in or proudly proclaiming as home?

What I have expressed or I am trying to say are feelings that over a billion Indians believe are true. It is almost as if these thoughts have become a common thread that binds the nation together. The voices of anger, frustration, grief and helplessness shouting 'it's really not possible to live in this country anymore', have become commonplace. Will this state of affairs ever change? Will the people ever be able to sigh with relief and feel confident that there is some hope in the future?

Strange as it may seem, unless one is a politician, a bureaucrat, a policeman, a corporate head, a judge, a smuggler, a black-marketer or a ubiquitous fixer, life is full of dejection, struggle and the perpetual fight to earn a decent living. For the so-called elite of the nation, life is a cakewalk, thanks to the various political connections they enjoy. For the rest, it's just a hopeless journey that they are forced to embark upon.

Have you ever thought about what it is that has reduced India to such lows? Why we experience such painful helplessness everyday, in every walk of life and in every possible way? Have you ever analysed why a billion Indian citizens find no hope in their own country even after six decades of being an independent and a self-reliant nation?

The answer is very short and simple!

Today, India is all about the selfishness of a few—those who live in the higher echelons of society and are the self-proclaimed protectors of the country. They smartly fool the entire population, courtesy their double-faced personalities and lack of scruples. The fact is that none of them serves the nation; they only serve their selfish interests. Sadly, there are plenty of them everywhere. In politics, in bureaucracy, in judiciary, in police, in business, in academics; you name a field and place and they are present. It is as if the nation is surviving on the basis a grand nexus that works on self-interest. Ethics, laws, decorum, character have all given way to selfishness and greed.

In a nutshell, it would not be incorrect to call India a nation 'of the nexus, by the nexus and for the nexus'. If you have built a nexus of your own, you can do everything. If you are out of it and live like a common citizen you have nothing.

It is this nexus that can free a criminal and can imprison the innocent.

It is this nexus that can give you a fake degree and can deny a seat to the most deserving.

It is this nexus that absolves a person who sells drugs in the name of medicine, and it is this nexus that can end your business no matter how ethically you run it.

It is this nexus that can save a corrupt clerk from serving time in prison, and it is this nexus that can suspend honest officer for no fault of his.

It is this nexus that can award you any contract, pushing aside ethics and transparency.

These are just few of the examples. The current state of the nation is so bad that one may run out of space to list them and still be surprised that there are many more left.

The police know which file to pick up and which one to overlook, whom to arrest and whom not to. The income tax officer knows whom to raid and whom to leave out. The doctors know whom to admit for treatment and whom not to give even the most basic first aid. The food and civil supply officers know how to pass adulterated and poisonous food and what not to allow even if it is healthy. The contractors know which engineer matters and which one does not. The lawyer knows which judge to socialize with and which one to ignore. The officer knows which minister can save him and who cannot. The minister knows which officer can help him loot more and who cannot. In fact, it is all thanks to this powerful nexus that a few have learnt how to survive and, therefore, confidently control, plunder, oppress and subjugate civil society.

If you notice how this network works, you will realize how professional and organized it is. Years of research and hardwork are put into studying the mindset, character, conduct, preferences, taste and other traits of the targeted. Meticulous planning goes into cultivating people of repute and power and in the process each of their demands are fulfilled, no matter how outlandish they be.

Some may want money, another a holiday in a luxurious resort on an exotic island, some demand plum postings or a cushy job while another craves exclusive properties the list goes on and on. And in the process of give and take and 'mutual understandings', every impossible becomes possible all in the name of 'share and care'.

Deals are sealed in posh clubs, bars and pubs or farmhouses rather than in offices. Tenders are made, customized and remade. Actions are taken or stopped, judgments are given or withheld, inquires are commissioned or withdrawn, promotions are awarded or demotions ordered, transfers are dispensed or stopped. Everything, almost everything is passed under the aegis of this powerful nexus.

It is this nexus that is today giving rise to endless corruption, nepotism, wrong doings, unlawful acts, immoral conducts and loss of morality, honesty or ethics. Sadly, it is only evolving and gaining strength with each passing day.

The people who are part of this nexus are thriving while others are rotting. The law, the judiciary, the government, the police only pander to the interests of those with vested powers. For everyone else there is just the hope that one day they will be able to break through the shackles of this nexus and make the nation and its citizens emerge stronger.

To file a complaint in police station, an ordinary citizen has to run from pillar to post to make his voice and problem heard, but the officers may or may not register the complaint. Years pass if you are a common man fighting a case. Most people drop out of it in the middle for want of proper hearing. Whether the result is in your favour or not you will still end up losing money and precious time and effort running helter-skelter through the corridors of the courts. Who should be held accountable for a common man's plight? Does living and surviving have to be such a painful struggle just because you are not part of some nexus or have not befriended a man of repute? Is India only a place for those with money and connections? We should bow our heads with shame if the answer is yes!

A certain section continues to twist the arm of law and the judiciary according to their wants and demands and all we can do is witness such a gory show. Each one of us should realize that the law and the country were not made for a selected few. We live in a democracy and everything we have belongs equally to all. By allowing some people to trample over our rights indicates a loss of dignity. By letting those with power become more powerful we are only signaling to them that they can continue to do what they want, while we sit blindfolded, like cowards, and allow the evil to take over.

Everyday the government which we elected is robbing us of our basic rights and we like fools are letting them do so. Take for example the case of government allotting huge areas of prime land to private schools for paltry sums on the condition that twenty-five per cent of the seats be reserved for the children from the economically weaker sections of society. But how many of these schools are fulfilling the condition? Their basic fees are so exhorbitant that even middle-class parents cannot afford to send their kids to such schools. Besides, how many underprivileged children do you see studying in these five-star private educational institutions? Do we as citizens not know this fact? Are we so unaware that we do not know what is happening in our own country? No we are not. We just like to pretend ignorance since raising a voice against injustice is not our cup of tea. We are ready to accept whatever is being forced upon us because our nation believes in tolerance and ahimsa, qualities that have been ingrained in our DNA for centuries.

Free land for schools is just one example, there are many who promise to build hospitals and other clinics in exchange for free services to the poor, but end up constructing plush medical facilities or townships where the poor are barred from entering. Clearly, how much is enough for these people in power? Is there ever going to be a limit which they will hit and say 'it's enough now'?

The fact is that these people do not care. They know there is no one above them who will question their greed and hold them accountable for their wrong doings. They are just a few powerful beasts that have been unleashed to devour the land of its beauty, wealth and resources.

If you try and understand the psyche of these people you

will know that they all share one common interest—their selfish nature and their insatiable desire for more. No matter how much they get, nothing is enough for them. In reality, these are the people who have taken the system into their hands and have monopolized and manipulated it. Maddened and massacred it. These are the people who have stifled the growth of the common and honest man and made his life miserable. In fact, these are the people who have the nation in their grip and are demeaning its glory and pride. They have killed the very idea of honest and truthful nation.

These people outnumber the sincere, ethical and good ones still left in the system, and what we fear right now is that these corrupt people will influence the honest few to become like them.

The questions that baffle us is for how long can we as an aspiring nation continue like this? For how long can a billion citizens remain subservient and oppressed by the nexus of the negatives? Can the nation ever be free of the shackles of the nexus?

The answer is—yes, the nation can. She surely can!

The nation currently is in grave need of people who can stand up against the system and restore faith in it once again. And for that we do not have to look far, because such qualities are inbuilt in each one of us. All we need is the right direction and guidance. Instead of pointing fingers at others, we need to look within ourselves and become self-sufficient enough to confront this nexus. Merely exposing them would not solve the problem. Killing its roots is the only solution to lay the foundation of a corruption- and greed-free nation. You and I will, and not a third party, have to unite in the fight against this evil. We need to be bold and daring. If we stand together, nothing can beat us. For the sake of our beloved nation, we should all come together and show the so-called powerful people that when an 'aam admi' decides to stand up for a cause he does not remain that 'aam'.

A Child's Cry

Poverty
Jane Taylor

I saw an old cottage of clay,
    And only of mud was the floor;
It was all falling into decay,
    And the snow drifted in at the door.

Yet there a poor family dwelt,
    In a hovel so dismal and rude;
And though gnawing hunger they felt,
    They had not a morsel of food.

The children were crying for bread,
    And to their poor mother they'd run;
'Oh, give us some breakfast,' they said,
    Alas! their poor mother had none.

She viewed them with looks of despair,
    She said (and I'm sure it was true),
''Tis not for myself that I care,
    But, my poor little children, for you.'

O then, let the wealthy and gay
    But see such a hovel as this,
That in a poor cottage of clay
    They may know what true misery is.

And what I may have to bestow
    I never will squander away,
While many poor people I know
    Around me are wretched as they.

They are born into God's world like you and me, but they seem to have fallen out of his grace. They are the future of the nation like all other children of India, but continue to live a deprived life because they are born in the family of the impoverished. And they will remain victims of this life forever. Is being born poor a curse?

Children are our future so what society or strata they are born into should not hamper their prospects for a better life ahead. If they are poor and lack the amenities, instead of shunning them we should provide them with what they deserve. They are the children of God as much as you and I are. We do not own Mother Earth and don't have the right to decide who should inhabit the planet and who should not.

Even the poor have dreams and desires and have a beating heart. Their desires might not be as lofty and elaborate as ours. For example, if we think of meals in five-star hotels, they think of one square meal a day; if we want to wear luxury brands, they want just enough to hide their modesty or keep warm in winters; if we dream of vacations abroad, they just want a pair of shoes so that they can protect their feet; for us cold water is a necessity, for them its any kind of water worth drinking. With such frugal desires and wants why can't we accept these little children as one of our own?

Little things give them immense happiness. A piece of cloth or a broken toy are what their memories are made of. They pick our leftovers from dustbins to satiate their hunger and sleep on pavements no matter what the weather is. For them a shelter in itself is a luxury. Now, if we compare their lives with that of our children, it seems there is a great divide. We often say 'it is not our mistake if they are born like this'. Agreed, it is no one's fault. Maybe it was destined for them to be born of lesser parents, but if we have the means, is it not our responsibility to help them grow in a better environment?

Just like we were not asked where we would like to be born, even these kids were not asked what kind of surroundings they would like to be born into. If it is not their fault that they were born into impoverished and deprived families, who are we to punish them and deprive them of their childhood?

A child is a child no matter what circumstances he or she is born into. At an age when they should be playing with friends, learning new things and enjoying life, many are forced to find ways to earn a livelihood. Poverty in our country has been cited as the major or root cause behind child labour. The 2001 national census of India estimated the total number of child labour, between the ages of five and fourteen, to be at 12.6 million. We often spot small children employed at roadside eateries or begging when they should actually be in school and studying. Their only crime is that they are born poor and hence learn to fend for themselves. Even we as noble citizens of the country do not take any steps to stop this injustice. For the children it is a necessity, but for us it should become a priority to stop such evils happening in front of our eyes.

Even though the government has introduced many stringent laws against child labour, ultimately it is up to us to put a stop to such practices. The government is set to debar employment of children below the age of fourteen in any industry; only those between fourteen and eighteen years can be employed, except in hazardous industries. The government needs to sensitize people on such matters. To rehabilitate such children and their families, it should open shelters, schools and create more means of livelihood for the parents so that their kids can go to school without worrying where the next meal will come from.

But it is not only the government's responsibility, we as mature and adult citizens must contribute to eradicate this evil. We should encourage people to share their books with underprivileged children, help them learn how to read and write, teach them, provide them with toys and items of necessity like food, medical aid, clean drinking water, clothes. These kids are not hungry just for money or food. Even they have desires and wishes which they hope to fulfil one day. For them life is just about meeting their most basic everyday needs. They may dream big but don't have the resources to fulfil them. They are just like you and me, only born in a different class. Try to bring a change in their lives so that they too can live a dignified existence. Be the guiding angel they are longing for and see how happy you can make them. Make a difference to the life of at least one child in your lifetime and you will notice how happy and content it will make you.

The Second Freedom Struggle

If

Rudyard Kipling

If you can keep your head when all about you
Are losing theirs and blaming it on you,
If you can trust yourself when all men doubt you,
But make allowance for their doubting too;
If you can wait and not be tired by waiting,
Or being lied about, don't deal in lies,
Or being hated, don't give way to hating,
And yet don't look too good, nor talk too wise:
If you can dream—and not make dreams your master,
If you can think—and not make thoughts your aim;
If you can meet with Triumph and Disaster
And treat those two impostors just the same;
If you can bear to hear the truth you've spoken
Twisted by knaves to make a trap for fools,
Or watch the things you gave your life to, broken,
And stoop and build 'em up with worn-out tools:
If you can make one heap of all your winnings
And risk it all on one turn of pitch-and-toss,
And lose, and start again at your beginnings
And never breathe a word about your loss;

If you can force your heart and nerve and sinew
To serve your turn long after they are gone,
And so hold on when there is nothing in you
Except the Will which says to them: "Hold on!"
If you can talk with crowds and keep your virtue,
Or walk with kings—nor lose the common touch,
If neither foes nor loving friends can hurt you,
If all men count with you, but none too much;
If you can fill the unforgiving minute
With sixty seconds' worth of distance run,
Yours is the Earth and everything that's in it,
And—which is more—you'll be a Man, my son!

The above poem not only motivates us to be brave and face the evil situations within and outside our mind, body and soul, but it is also a commentary on how we must go on with just one motto in mind 'The country shall prevail'.

Decades ago, there was a freedom struggle. A struggle, to be able to live with dignity. It was the struggle that changed the face of a nation and the lives of her citizens; it was the struggle for independence from the rule of oppression, deceit, oppressive laws and misdeeds of those in power. The time was the early 1900s. Decades later, in the 2000s, we are still fighting the same fight. Albeit not against foreign invaders but with our own people, people who claim to be our protectors and whom we voted for in the hope they would be our true friends and confidants.

Today, it seems as if we are once again embarking on yet another freedom struggle! The first one was the fight to free India from the British Raj. The second one is about the fight to free Indians from the clutches of the corrupt, dishonest, criminals and the mafia raj.

Then, there were brave hearts like Bhagat Singh, Rajguru, Azad and many more who faced death because they raised voices against the British.

Today, there are few in that league like Satyendra Dubey, who are either killed or threatened with dire consequences, whenever they dare raise alarm against the mafia raj.

Then, it was a foreign power that plundered our wealth and became richer.

Today, it is our own countrymen who are plundering our wealth left, right and centre and are becoming millionaires and billionaires overnight.

The time has come for the second freedom struggle to become more intense and forceful, so that finally the corrupt, the criminals, the dishonest politicians, bureaucrats, corporate houses and the mafias go to jail once and for all, or at least until we find a solution to their problem.

However, many of our countrymen, social activists, students, youth, housewives, farmers, professional and even some good, honest politicians are getting more conscious about the need for a bigger change and are working towards it.

There is a strong belief that this new generation and the empowered youth have more wisdom and the conviction to play a key role in changing the nation's destiny once and forever. I, too, trust our new generation and believe that if anybody can bring about an awakening, then it is the youth of the country. With their new age ideas, dedication, freshness of thoughts and views and the willingness to go that extra mile, they can truly make the difference.

They are more focused, self-motivated more assertive and open about raising their voice against injustice. They know what they want and they will do everything possible to achieve that.

If they join in the new freedom struggle, guided and encouraged by the right people at the helm, they can change the system and wash off any dirt.

And I know they will do that only if they strongly relate and connect to the problems.

I do believe that we need liberation from this system that has been crippling us in every way.

We need freedom from looters of our natural resources who even disobey court orders and plunder our mines for personal gains.

We need freedom from vote-buying practices that sell the country into the hands of the corrupt.

We need freedom from lazy, arrogant bureaucracy that wants everything without deserving anything.

We need freedom from the police system, which terrorizes the common man and panders to the high and the mighty.

We need freedom from adulterated food items, which are sold at the neighbourhood shops and lead to illness and death.

We need freedom from crimes committed in broad daylight and yet no security is ever extended to a common man.

And above all we need freedom from the pervading poverty, malnutrition, hunger and helplessness.

And finally, we need freedom from a stark difference between the growing India of the few and the ever-suffering Bharat of the millions.

Have we ever thought that what we have made of our country is contrary to our forefathers' dream of an independent India? Have we ever thought about what exactly we wanted or struggled for to achieve freedom from? If the country was to rot like this today, why did our forefathers die fighting for her freedom?

With decades of constant degeneration in political and value systems, courtesy a few thousand politicians, bureaucrats, businessmen, criminals and fixers, we have lost our India of the past once again. While they are free to loot the country at their will with no one stopping them or controlling their greed, we have lost faith in everything.

And on the other side, there are millions of rural farmers,

poor labourers, working classes who struggle just to eat and live. While a few thousands are becoming billionaires taking benefits of our much-hyped growth index, the rest are just struggling to live. Is it so that when India gained independence, Bharat did not?

Though this may sound terrible, can anyone give an answer as to why there are two countries in one?

Why Bharat suffers and hardly grows while India makes global headlines for its growth story?

What is this? Why? And how long will it last?

So should the billions of India, that is Bharat, celebrate the Independence Day on the next 15 August?

Should they boycott it?

Should they go on fast?

Should they protest?

The real citizens of India must declare their second freedom struggle with full force and work hard for it till we completely mitigate the cruel differences between a rising India and a falling Bharat, and build a new, clean, effective system and a country that brings smiles to all.

Let us all be the fierce fighters of the second freedom struggle. Let us transform ourselves into genuine crusaders for the total emancipation of the Self.

Speak-Up to Ease-Up

The reality today is that we are all interdependent and have to coexist on this small planet. Therefore, the only sensible and intelligent way of resolving differences and clashes of interests, whether between individuals or nations, is through dialogue.

—*The Dalai Lama*

A proper dialogue is the best solution when dealing with controversies, so much so that even foes can become friends.

History is filled with acts of cruelty that has caused pain and anguish to the masses. Take for example dictators like Saddam, Gaddaffi or Charles Taylor, who has been sentenced to fifty years' imprisonment for atrocities committed in Sierra Leone during the 1990 Civil War. While delivering justice the distinguished judge observed: 'Leadership must be carried out by examples, by the prosecution of crimes, not the commission of crimes.'

Have you ever thought about what leads to such inhuman and autocratic behaviour and what its eventual consequences are? It is the absence of the belief that dialogue can lead to peaceful coexistence and a better world for all.

Yes, it is only dialogue that can break barriers, bridge gaps and build the base for mutual understanding that will lead to a sensible conclusion to any crisis.

Dialogue is the key to speaking out, touching hearts and winning minds.

Unfortunately, however, there are still some people who

believe that domination and ruling with an iron fist will keep them in power and suppress all opposition. They are not interested in the exchange of views or opinions. As a result, as history has shown us, the path they have followed will ultimately lead to their downfall.

Have you ever analysed why this is so?

It is very simple. A despot, even though he is all-powerful and dominating, eventually cannot withstand the anger of the people he has suppressed so harshly. It is the power of the many that can destroy the power of one or a few. This is also the law of nature.

Solving issues through dialogue benefits ordinary individuals as much as it does nations and leaders. When you consider the value of dialogue in daily life you will be convinced by how necessary it is for making life more peaceful.

A disagreement between husband and wife, son, daughter, colleague or boss can easily be solved through dialogue. But if you assume that 'what I think is right' then, most probably, you will annoy family and friends, and eventually run the risk of losing them.

To thrust your will and views on others is autocratic, whereas dialogue is democratic. Thus, dialogue is an effective tool to understand and appreciate another's point-of-view.

Do you know why dictators or autocrats consider it their right to behave the way they do? It is because dialogue has no role to play in their world. As a result, reality finally catches up with them, ultimately leading to their downfall.

So friends, no matter whether you score high or low on your relationship barometer—with parents, family, friends, lovers, colleagues—begin or continue to indulge in a healthy dialogue so that the relationship gets stronger and stronger.

In personal life or social life, in business or politics, dialogue is the essence that keeps any relationship alive, whatever the circumstances. So whenever there are roadblocks, just start a dialogue and see how the problems vanish!

That is the beauty of democracy. That is the beauty of living life with an open mind.

More Power to Woman Power

For most of history, Anonymous was a woman.
—*Virginia Woolf*

In the twenty-first century, one often hears much-hyped statements like 'woman on top' and terms like 'gender equality', signifying the change in the status of women in society. However, in reality, this is still very much a man's world. Except for a few countries or societies, women are still subservient to men and are treated as such. Men have always had double standards when it comes to women, with one set of rules for men and another for women.

In India, women have always been considered the weaker sex, even though we have the maximum number of female gods—Durga, Radha, Saraswati, Vaishno Devi—whom we worship. Yet, women are discriminated upon. The 2011 Census Report reveals the disparity in the country's man—woman ratio, which also indicates that female infanticide continues unabated. The population as per its provisional figures is 1210.19 million of which 623.7 million (51.54 per cent) are males and 586.46 million (48.46 per cent) are females.

Alarming isn't it? Why is this so?

Let's face it.

A man can wear anything he likes, but a woman's choice is dictated by the norms of society and its custodians.

A son can go out with whomsoever he chooses and return

home late at night, but if a daughter does the same, her freedom is curbed.

Take marriage as an example. A girl is required to pass a series of tests before she is considered suitable, but boys have no such obligations. Instead, it is their prerogative to accept or reject a proposal.

A girl is examined almost as if she's a milch cow. She is subjected to several embarrassing questions like: 'what's your weight', 'when did you start wearing spectacles?', 'can you cook?', 'do you like English movies' and so on. Besides the barrage of questions, she is also judged by how she walks, how she serves tea, is she soft-spoken or not. We should be thankful that she is not expected to pass the virginity test!

What is even more disheartening for the girl is that she has to go through the same questioning drill until she is deemed 'fit' by someone. No one bothers about the girl's feeling. In the name of tradition, we make our daughters and sisters demonstrate their suitability, and subject them to the possibility of rejection and humiliation.

What kind of mindset is this? Why are boys not subjected to the same treatment? Do we still think of girls as a burden?

The reality is far from it. In most cases, it has been observed that women are smarter than men. In many fields, too, they outshine their male colleagues. They manage the home efficiently, carefully plan and execute monthly budgets, look after the family. Moreover, they are more patient, stable, compassionate, sincere, dutiful and dedicated both at home and at work. In fact, they are the home minister and finance minister, but can never become prime minister because the family will not elect them for that position.

In other words, they are the stronger sex, though unfortunately have been termed as the weaker sex.

When will women be treated with dignity? When will they

enjoy the freedom they deserve?

Thank God, modern women have shown the courage and conviction to prove their worth in every possible way and have also brought about a change in the way they are seen and perceived.

But is that enough?

Be it the educated or the illiterate, the rich or poor, the story of women is the same everywhere, be it in India, the US or the UK. How long will this continue? And how long will it take for men to realize their potential and accept them as equals, if not betters?

Another decade, another century, another millennium?

A nation and society can only develop and mature if it learns to respect women and to give them the rights they deserve.

It is up to us to build the kind of society we want for ourselves and future generations. A society where both men and women are equal.

Euthanasia:
A Blessing or a Curse?

Life is a gift from god, and is sacred. Dying cannot be decided by another person. So are we saying 'right to life is okay, but right to death is not?'

The case of the fifty-nine-year-old Aruna Shanbaug sparked off a heated debate across India. Aruna was a nurse at Mumbai's King Edward Memorial Hospital (KEM) when she was brutally raped in 1973. As a result of that traumatic experience she went into a coma from which she has never recovered. With no relatives by her side, she has been lying in a permanent vegetative state in the same hospital she worked for some thirty-six years. Her primary caregivers are the hospital staff who have tended to her needs selflessly.

In 2010 journalist, Pinky Virani, filed a petition for mercy killing, stating that no human being should be forced to live a life stripped of basic dignity. This led to a nation-wide debate on whether euthanasia should be legalized. While the merits and demerits are still being discussed, the question here is: who decides when to end a life? The person who is in a coma or the caregiver or doctors or the law or the citizens?

Euthanasia is a Greek word meaning good death, and is also referred to as mercy killing. Even though it is legal in just three countries—the Netherlands, Belgium and Luxembourg—efforts to change policies have met with limited or no success elsewhere in the world.

On 7 March 2011, while turning down Pinki Virani's plea to allow euthanasia for Aruna, the Supreme Court observed that Pinki Virani cannot be treated as next of friend, since that status can only be given to her team of caregivers at KEM Hospital. However, the Court gave legal status to passive euthanasia, allowing the withdrawal of life support of a patient in permanent vegetative state, and stated: 'A decision has to be taken to discontinue life support either by the parents or the spouse or other close relatives, or in the absence of any of them, such a decision can be taken even by a person or a body of persons acting as a next friend. It can also be taken by the doctors attending the patient. However, the decision should be taken bona fide in the best interest of the patient.'

In India, life and death are sacred matters. A human or any other life form is celebrated equally, whether in life or death. To accept the fact that another person has the right to decide whether someone should live or die, will take time. Keeping such attitudes in mind, it is understandable why policy-makers believe that mercy killing should not be allowed. Besides there is also the hope that the patient may miraculously recover at some time.

Medical science has yet to find a cure for terminal illnesses like HIV/AIDS, cancer and several others. In many cases the patient is reduced to a vegetative state, unaware of bodily functions or the world around him/her. It is in such situations that people take refuge in God and hope for miracles to happen and that our loved one will recover. Accepting death even if it occurs naturally is difficult to comprehend, so can we really consent to mercy killing?

While some people feel that mercy killing will free the patient from the indignity of his/her situation, the family will refuse to accept this harsh reality, and hope that doctors will find a cure. And so, the patient survives on life-support systems for as long as possible.

The question then arises that under what circumstances should mercy killing be allowed and legalized? Perhaps if a patient makes an appeal? Or if both the patient and family mutually agree? The first right should always be the patient's because it is his/her life after all, while the family's is second, since they are the caregivers and are more familiar with the patient's condition.

But legal issues aside, when I think like an Indian I question the morality behind euthanasia.

Why just Aruna? There are many like her in our country who are afflicted by organ failure, incurable diseases and old age. Should we leave them to suffer until nature takes her course? Do they not deserve to die with dignity? Hope is positive, but hoping against hope is foolhardy.

We are still not mature enough to make euthanasia legal. Besides, the biggest fear is that it could be misused rather than serve its rightful purpose. We feel that a person has the right to live and that he/she should also have the right to die with dignity. But it must be left to God, because only he can decide about life or death.

A Mission Before Us

India is more about simplicity and humility, but it is fast becoming complex and arrogant. Are the changing times pointing towards an alarming period ahead?

The arrogance displayed by the top brass and rich shows that India today is nothing but a reflection of how our values have eroded over time. Misbehaviour in public spaces has unfortunately become the standard behaviour of those in power even if it is absolutely unnecessary.

The ever growing socioeconomic divide could be one of the reasons, but to me it looks more like the callous attitude of the people around us that has led to such problems. There is absolutely no respect for the Constitution or the political system, the law or the judiciary. It is only money that matters and has become the god of the nation.

I often hear people saying: How dare you look at me like this? How dare you talk to me in a loud voice? Do you know who I am?

They act and talk as though they are either God or even a higher entity. Ordinary citizens are killed in road rage, journalists are threatened if they write an expose, police are pressurised, honest bureaucrats and police officers are transferred for the crime of doing their duty correctly, poor farmers and landowners are the victims of the land mafia, who buy their properties at low rate. All these things are part of everyday life; thanks to the wealthy few who have the means.

Even at home, when you ask your son why he has come

home so late, he will reply: 'Why are you asking such a question? How dare you?'

You can't even ask your daughter these days. You can't talk to your spouse, grandfather or grandchildren. You can't question politicians, bureaucrats or businessmen. Society has become arrogant, insensitive, intolerant.

Yes, my friends, you will realize that at every step and in every walk of life, something disturbing is happening, quite contrary to our great culture and tradition of truth, humility, simplicity and selfless service.

Where will this erosion of values lead us to?

It has already weakened our faith in honesty, integrity and the law, as we see how the corrupt, the rich and mighty and the mafia get away with crime after crime with no regard for the law.

It has already created a dangerous attitude that money can buy everyone and everything.

If someone says something to you, just hit him. Most probably, you shall be charged under IPC 325, which is a bailable offence. In this way, Bollywood stars, rich children of even richer parents, politicians, industrialists and bureaucrats go scot-free. Evidently, the law is for the poor and not for the rich.

This is shameful. What kind of law is this?

One that only works in India!

But for how long can this new (trackless) India afford to be a silent spectator? Only you can answer that. After all, India is yours. And you, the youth, have to set it right.

Let Creativity Be!

The death of the legendary painter and filmmaker M.F. Hussain has left a huge void in the world of creative art. But what was even more heartbreaking was that he died in exile, in a land he did not consider his home, but which still accepted him with respect.

Hussain was forced to leave India because of a small group of religious fanatics, who were baying for his blood for portraying Hindu deities in what some considered a disrespectful manner, and a non-bailable warrant and fatwa were issued, which forced him to take shelter in Qatar in 2006. Since then he had harboured a wish to visit his beloved motherland at least once in his lifetime. But all in vain.

His situation was a sad commentary on the democratic morals of a nation which did not have the courtesy to protect him from the ire of some religious groups. Art is a creative medium and what artists depict on canvas or in a book are their own individual expression and not that of the nation or a group of people. One should learn to be tolerant to artistic expressions and not use them to entice communal hatred. After all, we live in a democratic nation and our thinking should be reflective of those values.

The world is full of so-called moral police, but the question is who gives them the authority to decide what is right and what is wrong? The means that they apply through demonstrations, the burning of effigies, issuing death threats and vandalism are destructive, so how can they blame someone of hurting the sentiments of others?

When people like M.F. Hussain or Taslima Nasreen or Salman Rushdie are forced to take refuge in other countries, it's a shame on a nation's political and social fabric. Surely in a country of billions, one man or a woman should be allowed freedom of expression without religious groups braying for their blood and issuing threats. Instead, they go scot-free as there is no system to keep them and their rowdy behaviour under control.

Not every person is born with the gift of creativity. But those who are should be given full freedom to express their emotions and feelings. However, this freedom of expression should be within limits. At the same time, people should be tolerant about great works of art and literature. When an Indian becomes an international celebrity, no matter how distantly he is related to the country, we laud his achievements, claiming that he has made the country proud. Yet, at the same time, we shun the very same people who produced such world famous works. What double standards are these?

Creative people are free souls. They belong to no religion, no country and to no one. For them what they create is their religion, caste and identity. So how can they be accused of hurting someone's sentiments?

Their art should be viewed in this perspective only—as belonging to no one.

My heart fills with sorrows when I think how M.F. Hussain would have felt before he died.

Was he thinking of India and his time spent here? Did he feel abandoned by a system that could not protect him? Was he thinking about the fundamentalists who forced him out of his own land? Did he wish to be born again in the country that shunned him at such a crucial phase of his life, even though he had given this land all his talent and art?

These questions often disturb me as I know I can never find answers to them. But I will always remember him as the man who portrayed India extravagantly as a vibrant and beautiful land. And yet, tragically, he died in exile because of his great love for his nation.

Three Monkeys are Still Around!

A teenage girl was raped in a moving vehicle. Nobody saw it while it was happening. The income tax officer built five palatial buildings. Nobody saw it. The BDO of the block took all the food packets for the poor to sell. Again, nobody saw it. Question papers of top institutions like IIT are leaked. No one knew how or when they reached the students. The police thrashed an innocent person in public who later died. Nobody raised a voice. The doctor left a pair of scissors in the stomach of a woman who later died . Nobody raised an alarm. The trader sold adulterated milk for high profits. Nobody, even the civil supply officer, saw it. The income tax officer's wife had twelve bank deposits. Nobody knew.

The now infamous Coalgate happened with full political knowledge, yet nobody claims to have been party to it. Worse, most files related to the case have also vanished into thin air.

Just imagine how easy it is for people to feign innocence and ignorance once their sins are exposed. It then becomes a case of passing the buck. The circus goes on till a new case is unearthed and the previous is pushed into the background. When issues are fresh in public memory every case is followed with avid interest, once it fades no one knows what happened to those involved and if the guilty ever paid for their crimes. Criminal and political conspiracies continue to take place and the nation is continuously being robbed of its wealth, dignity and resources.

Do we still exist as a nation?

Are we still living like noble and responsible citizens?

Are we, as a nation, really growing and moving towards a bright future?

God save us if your answer is no!

The main concern is that our apathy has probably made us unaware of the dangers and disasters ahead.

If we are aware of the wrongs that are happening around us, why are we being so ambiguous? Why are we deaf, dumb and blind? So much so that the nation bleeds while we stand still and plead in vain. Why are we shy of calling a spade a spade?

The main reason, my friends, is that I think that we are following Mahatma Gandhi's approach to what's happening around us. The lesson of see no evil, talk no evil, hear no evil as explained to us through the three monkeys, each depicting one facet. Gandhiji propagated this valuable lesson during the freedom struggle to tell the people that even if the British broke your spirit do not let them deviate you from the path to freedom. Do not get provoked if they upbraid you or beat your comrades. No matter what they do don't answer back. The virtues of patience and ignorance were tactics used by Indians to frustrate the British and break their will.

So though we see a crime or a corruption, we don't really see it. We hear about criminals and the mafia taking advantage of our country and its systems, but we hardly complain. Neither do we speak or protest to save the nation. Because our Mahatma has taught us not to hear even if the message is loud and clear. However, what we tend to forget is that what was applicable in those days cannot work today. Instead, we follow the message blindly without understanding its true meaning and context.

The moral of the three monkeys' tale does not have any meaning today. We are not fighting for our freedom from an external power. The enemy lies within our country in the form of our own fellow Indians and being blind, deaf and mute to the evils in society will leave us helpless and insecure. We have to fight the evil. Speak up and punish those who are guilty. We have to take matters into our hands and teach the corrupt the lessons they deserve.

Each one of us must voice our opinions strongly and denounce every wrong deed. We owe a lot to our motherland, which means that it is our duty to prevent politicians and bureaucrats from killing our democratic spirit. For how long can we tolerate the wrongs that are taking place and celebrate the guilty? Now the time has come that all conspirators should be made to realize that they will have to pay for their misdeeds. Our future and that of the country lies in our hands and we alone must decide her destiny. We must not let the greedy and corrupt decide for us.

Let us stand together and change our own nation for better. Our country is in trouble and who can come forward to save her?

Naturally WE! Yes, only WE!

Our nation is our responsibility and we will nurture her as a parent. Let us pledge to unite and fight against the evils. Not as disciples of the three monkeys but as responsible and concerned citizens.

Let our mission and thinking drive us on. Not the three monkeys.

To the Awakened India
Swami Vivekanand

Once more awake!
For sleep it was, not death, to bring thee life
Anew, and rest to lotus-eyes for visions
Daring yet. The world in need awaits, O Truth!
No death for thee!
Resume thy march,
With gentle feet that would not break the
Peaceful rest even of the roadside dust
That lies so low. Yet strong and steady,
Blissful, bold, and free. Awakener, ever
Forward! Speak thy stirring words.
Thy home is gone,
Where loving hearts had brought thee up and
Watched with joy thy growth. But Fate is strong—
This is the law—all things come back to the source
They sprung, their strength to renew.
Then start afresh
From the land of thy birth, where vast cloud-belted
Snows do bless and put their strength in thee,
For working wonders new. The heavenly
River tune thy voice to her own immortal song;
Deodar shades give thee eternal peace.
And all above,
Himala's daughter Umâ, gentle, pure,

The Mother that resides in all as Power
And Life, who works all works and
Makes of One the world, whose mercy
Opens the gate to Truth and shows
The One in All, give thee untiring
Strength, which is Infinite Love.
They bless thee all
The seers great, whom age nor clime
Can claim their own, the fathers of the
Race, who felt the heart of Truth the same,
And bravely taught to man ill-voiced or
Well. Their servant, thou hast got
The secret—'tis but One.

Then speak, O love!
Before thy gentle voice serene, behold how
Visions melt and fold on fold of dreams
Departs to void, till Truth and Truth alone
In all its glory shines—

And tell the world—
Awake, arise, and dream no more!
This is the land of dreams, where Karma
Weaves unthreaded garlands with our thoughts
Of flowers sweet or noxious, and none
Has root or stem, being born in naught, which
The softest breath of Truth drives back to
Primal nothingness. Be bold, and face
The Truth! Be one with it! Let visions cease,
Or, if you cannot, dream but truer dreams,
Which are Eternal Love and Service Free.

No Space for the Poor Here!

One look at our government-operated healthcare facilities will make us realize that we have a long way to go before we can call ourselves developed. The dismal condition of this sector suggests that the nation has become anti-poor. Government hospitals are overcrowded; private hospitals are beyond the reach of the poor. The state of healthcare in rural India is quite alarming and suggests a serious failure at the planning level and calls for the revamping of the entire system. This has to start by bringing transparency at all levels of decision making.

The poor of India bear the brunt of this sorry state of affairs. Those who can afford to pay buy themselves royal treatment, while those who cannot are shooed away by the very people who had pledged to save lives at any cost. This trend of ignoring the poor is alarmingly disturbing and, sadly, on the rise.

India spends just 4 per cent of its GDP on health. This has led to a very high out-of-pocket (OOP) expenditure for the general public.

Country	Total percentage of GDP spent on healthcare	Private expenditure percentage	Per capita spent on healthcare (US$)	Per capita government spends on healthcare (US$)
India	4.1	70.8	132	39
USA	17.9	46.9	8362	4437

The private medical sector remains the primary source of health care for 70 per cent of households in urban areas and 63 per cent of households in rural areas. Hence, it is hardly surprising that the private sector currently has 80 per cent of all doctors. Private hospitals are proliferating today mainly because people want better services. Sadly, patients are being exploited by these hospitals. Here we must not overlook the fact that these private hospitals take land at very subsidized prices from the government and build money-making entities. The government provides them with land on the conditions that a percentage of the beds will be kept aside for the poor and that they should be provided with quality treatment. But these norms are being shamelessly violated and openly flouted.

The truth is that this nation today has become a land of health business, corporate profits, merchant doctors, EMI-driven patient care for a chosen few. This private healthcare system is both insensitive and very expensive. The way such hospitals operate need to be scrutinized and publicized.

These are not hospitals, they are a bizarre patient bazaar of the worst kind. You will find only rich paymasters. Supposing a patient who is poor walks in, he is forced to cough up all that he has or all he can manage, it doesn't matter if he has to sell his property in order to buy health for himself.

These private hospitals are not just hospitals, they are also what I call 'mini malls' which allure patients as well as their visitors. While the patient gets treated in fully air-conditioned environs, attended by expensive doctors and sophisticated machinery, the family members can wander around, savour the feasts at the glitzy food bar—Chinese, Continental, north Indian, south Indian. In some cases, the private hospitals become a celebration venue for the rich patient and his family and kids. If you are not a foodie, you can listen to music, play video games, watch movies on widescreen television sets in artistically decorated public spaces, or simply hangout at the many fancy joints! And what a choice of rooms—ordinary, deluxe, semi-deluxe, super-deluxe, maharaja suite. For people with wealth, it does not matter if the cost go into lakhs of rupees; after all, some of this money might have been amassed overnight through scams or just good old everyday corruption.

But this is not my only fear about our flawed policies. We have many flaws that prove to be fatal. We still don't have a policy that makes it mandatory for doctors to spend few compulsive years in rural India, to care for the poor, keep them healthy and build a healthy base of human resources. We still allow all subsidized healthcare and benefits to those who can buy the best of world class healthcare for any small aliment, just because they are well-connected.

But what about the ordinary people? The poor majority is suffering and dying.

This great divide is making our nation sicker day by day.

The situation has not improved even though our courts advised private hospitals to reserve 25 per cent of poor patients and offer them free treatment. But no judgement of any court has any effect on them, but surely one day God's judgement will catch up with them.

What are we up to? Are we serious about building a healthy nation? Or we are more determined to save Europe than our poor?

Well, you may ask, why suddenly this inference? Yes, there is a reason. To show to the outside world that we are a financial power, recently our government donated many billion euros to some European nations to aid them in the recovery from the economic slump. Imagine a nation where the sick and poor are dying by the millions, and yet we are donating thousands of crores. Just to show the world our rich face. Or we are determined to save the rich of the world and let the poor continue to die—here in our own country or in some dark corners of Africa or elsewhere.

We have a very high child mortality rate, because of lack of nutrition that must be given to mother and child after birth. The absence of adequate medical facilities in the villages is another reason.

The current healthcare situation suggests that it is a curse to be born poor. Till the deprived section of a society is healthy, no nation can succeed in its quest to be a superpower. There is no contradicting the fact that the true prosperity of a nation can be or should be judged by the state of the health of its inhabitants.

In all certainty an effective network concerning health issues will be the most desirable thing here. The implementation of these should be expedited. Such an approach is sure to bring about a qualitative change in this country on the one hand and on the other, it will strengthen the democratic forces.

A Travesty of Democracy

People shouldn't be afraid of their government. Governments should be afraid of their people.

—Alan Moore

The biggest irony of democracy is that, on the one hand, it promotes freedom of all kinds, and yet on the other, it curbs your very right of expression. If you dare to open your mouth, you can land in trouble. Yes, I am talking about the controversy involving Kiran Bedi, Om Puri and Aseem Trivedi during the movement against corruption headed by Anna Hazare. It is true that their controversial remarks and attack on Parliament and the Constitution were uncalled for, but as citizens of a democratic country they have every right to express themselves. When the Constitution has given us the right to freedom of expression, who are we to decide who says what, when and where.

Everyone will agree that the days of the great leaders are gone. And today, the floors of Parliament are stained by the corrupt motives of corrupt leaders. I know that this is a harsh statement, but who does not know that many who sit in that citadel of democracy have very low moral characters and long records of crime and corruption.

The logic is clear and simple. If you are good and selfless you command respect.

If you are selfish and bad you don't get it, even if you demand it. That is exactly the situation here.

Where are those great selfless, visionary leaders who use to adorn our high house of democracy—our esteemed parliament?

People like Jawaharlal Nehru, Ram Manohar Lohia, Madhu Limaye, Madhu Dandavate, Vajpayee are respected even today, years after they have gone. Why, because they deserved it and followed the motto of country before self. Their conduct adhered to high democratic ideals and the real spirit of service. They are the ones who set examples by practising what they taught. Today's leaders are a far cry from their predecessors. They are corrupt, arrogant, selfish and more concerned about their personal wealth than that of the nation and her citizens. For them democracy means suppressing the truth and those who speak it. Taking away people's right to freedom of expression by branding them anti-national is the approach they apply. They arrest those who dare to speak against them. Sedation charges are slapped on those who try to reveal the truth and make the public aware of the reality. Talk against the Members of Parliament and you run the risk of being jailed. Speak against judges and you are accused of contempt of court.

So where will the public go? Will they live in perpetual fear of not expressing their views even if they have a point to make? How can citizens on whom the whole edifice of democracy stand be so helpless? How can the pillars of democracy—legislature, judiciary and the media thrive if their very foundations are left at the mercy of a few? Where is democracy in our country? Why is it that only a handful of people have the clout that gives them the right to redesign the very foundation on which this country was established? Who gave them this right? I do not say that taking advantage of democracy should be allowed, or that people should be encouraged to do whatever they wish, but then, neither should one oppress another. To each his own, and if it is one person's point of view then let it not become that of millions of others. And if these so called protectors of the country are so bothered about their image being tarnished, why don't they look within themselves instead of pointing fingers at others? Our politicians, because of their questionable character and conduct, have lost the moral authority to expect decorum, even though they think it their due.

What the aforementioned people did was definitely not acceptable, but then why commit deeds that provoke people to speak ill of you at public platforms? Instead of moral policing, these leaders and bureaucrats must shun their personal likings and needs and look after the interest of those who bring them to power. It is a democratic nation, yes, but right to expression does not mean looting the country of its resources and filling one's bank balance, neither does it mean speaking ill of each other.

Disabled or Differently Abled?

We, the one's who are challenged, need to be heard. To be seen not as a disability, but as a person who has, and will continue to bloom. To be seen not only as a handicap, but as a well intact human being.
—*Robert M. Hensel*

Disability is a widespread stigma in our country. In every state, district and corner of town, we come across people who suffer from some form of disability or the other, some are crippled or deaf or mute, others blind or suffering from polio or are mentally challenged or rendered disabled because of health-related problems. The fact remains that there is a sizeable number of disabled people in our country, yet we remain ignorant about them and their needs. More than two crores people suffer from various disabilities in the country, including ten million blind. Just Uttar Pradesh alone is home to thirty-five lakhs such people.

Despite these glaring numbers, are we as a country, sensitive enough towards our disabled population? Are the government and other authorities and institutions doing what is required to make us receptive towards our differently-abled population? Do we have enough facilities and reforms in place to help them live a life of dignity and respect?

Malnutrition has been a major problem in the country and it has also been cited as the major reason for children suffering from cerebral palsy or other mental disorders. According to the data collected by UN Enable, there are close to twelve million children in India who suffer from disabilities and of that approximately eight per cent fall under the mentally challenged category.

Nutrition deficiency during pregnancy, premature delivery, communicable diseases, early motherhood, interfamily marriages, insufficient access to medical facilities, poor sanitation, post-birth complications, genetic history, are some of the reasons why children suffer from disabilities at birth. In a country which boasts of sound economic reforms and an increasing number of people entering the billion dollar club, it is a shame to know that there is still a large chunk of our population comprising children who don't even get a proper meal or clean environs to be healthy. Does their condition not concern the country's well-heeled and high-flyers? Or is it that their charitable causes and donations are limited to the publicity they receive for Page 3 events?

Imagine the plight of the families below poverty line when they give birth to a child with some type of physical or mental deformity, they are already reeling under the burden of poverty, and neither have the money nor the resources to look after such kids. As a result they are either abandoned at birth or left to die by their helpless families. It is estimated that only one per cent of such children have access to special schools. Lack of infrastructure and high cost of living, which includes medical expenses, a 24X7 helper and other necessities, force parents to choose otherwise. The social and economic burdens are at times too onerous for a family to handle.

Our country also does not have a very disable-friendly infrastructure. I have seen people on wheelchairs and crutches struggling to navigate malls, movie halls, airports or on to public transports. Schools, universities and other academic institutions do not have the facilities to accommodate blind or physically challenged students, which deprives many of them from higher education. The schools meant for the differently abled are few and have their own issues and restrictions to deal with. Compared to the conditions in the West, our country still has a long way to go to become a disable-friendly nation.

The 2001 census estimated that close to 2.13 per cent of the total population, or around twenty-five million, suffered from various physical anomalies. Since then the numbers have gone up considerably, yet there has been little change in the way we treat our disabled people. The mindset remains the same as we view them as a burden on society, and by ostracizing them from communities and gatherings we feel that we have washed our hands off the responsibility. The government needs to further strengthen its drive for the cause of the disabled. More schools and training institutes, specially trained teachers, free or subsidized medical aid, disable-friendly walkways and toilets in public spaces, campaigns to sensitize the masses at large towards such people are some of the positive solutions that need to be put into place immediately.

They don't just want schools and institutes, they demand attention and care. These people are called 'differently abled' because even though they might come across as physically deformed, they have reflexes and senses which work better than any average human being. Their sense of smell, feel, touch, memory and such forth, are at times, intimidating, and their talents need to be developed with patience. Had it not been for someone's patience people like Stephen Hawkins, Louis Braille, Stevie Wonder, John Milton, Beethoven, Albert Einstein and others, would not have overcome their disability to enlighten us with their mental strength and special gifts in their respective fields of science, music, literature and the arts.

By spending time with them, and most importantly, accepting them as one of us we can do them great service. Helping the blind cross the road or spending a weekend or a month at a school for the mentally or physically challenged, organizing benefit shows or giving them a chance to perform at various public platforms, helping them get the right education and developing skills that will make them self-dependent are some of the things we can do to make them feel special and accepted.

The youth of today are not slaves to archaic thinking nor do they endorse any kind of inequality in society. Therefore, such young professionals can play a vital role in bringing about a change in atititude towards the physically challenged. With the help of the social networks they can create groups which can contribute in taking the cause of disability further. They can become spokespeople for many such forums and encourage people to start treating the disabled as humans.

It takes a lot of effort and patience to shape the life of a human, especially when he/she is deprived in some way or the other. As able and physically normal humans, it becomes our duty to rise above our prejudices and create an environment where people are not denied basic amenities just because they have physical shortcomings. A loss of limb or sight or hearing or speech should not be the yardstick to judge the ability of a person or his/her character. We need to let them bloom as no one knows what special gifts they have that might benefit mankind.

There is no doubt that by giving them our love and acceptance we will only expand our own abilities. They don't need any eleemosynary supplies of goods. What they really want is a sympathetic understanding of their existence.

Stop Killing the Girl Child!

India has been independent for more than sixty years, yet some people are still trapped in age-old thoughts and beliefs regarding the 'girl–boy' inequality. It appears as if 'liberal' Indian has failed to change the other orthodox India. Superficially, it is true that India is progressing, but in reality the picture is not as vibrant; in fact, it is grim especially in the context of how we treat the fairer sex.

The status of women in a country as vast as ours is unfortunately something to be sympathetic about. Although we are an advancing nation, the practise of killing the unborn girl child that is still prevalent not only in the rural areas but in metros too, pushes us back into the Dark Ages. Narrow-minded people perpetuate such practises because they see a girl child as a burden and they don't want to cope with the expenses of rearing her. It is shocking to even think that even in the twenty-first century people think about such petty things.

Many families pressurize women to give birth to boys, in spite of knowing that this is a natural process. They believe that a boy will take the family's name forward, light the funeral pyre and be the breadwinner. But today, are girls less competent than boys? All around us are examples that women are equal to, if not better, than men. They always top the school board examinations, they are born mangers, hold top positions in corporate, medical, banking and other professions. So how can they be any less than men?

According to the 2011 census, the number of girls stands

at 940 which is a marginal increase from 933 in 2001. Not surprisingly, Haryana has the lowest sex ratio among the states while Kerala remains at the top with the highest. In the national capital Delhi, the statistics stand at 821 girls against 1,000 boys in 2001 compared to 866 in 2011. According to the statistics, nearly ten million female foetuses have been aborted in the country over the past two decades. Of the twelve million girls born in India, one million do not see their first birthdays.

Everyday we hear of incidents of female foetus found lying wrapped up in bags and thrown in dustbins. It just shows how rampant the problem is and how, despite the changing scenario, people have not changed their thinking regarding females. The government has, over the years, brought in many stringent laws to deal with the problem. A ban on sex determination is one such law that has been introduced, yet there are numerous hospitals and clinics which do it and are ready to abort the child on the parents' insistence for as little as Rs 5,000. Consider the role of the doctor, whose aim is to save lives, yet happily kills the foetus for a mere two thousand bucks! What is more heartwrenching is the fact that the aborted foetuses are often fed to dogs.

For most doctors, this is a clandestine operation, but what is tragic is that the killing takes place in the open, yet no one raises a voice against it. Mere laws will not curb the problem. Implementing them ruthlessly can be a solution. The United Nations' World Population Fund has indicated that India has one of the highest sex imbalances in the world. Not surprisingly, demographers warn that there will be a shortage of brides in the next twenty years because of the adverse juvenile sex ratio, combined with an overall decline in fertility. What a sorry state the country will be in the future if we continue to commit such crimes against a gender whom we otherwise lovingly worship and seek blessings from.

Think of women like Indira Gandhi, Sarojni Naidu, Mother

Teresa, Naina Lal Kidwai, Sonia Gandhi, Saina Nehwal and many more—they are women who have, in their own capacity, made the country proud. Do we consider them inferior or does their talent diminish just because they were born girls? No! There was someone, somewhere, who gave them the right to life and nurtured them to reach a status where we all look up to them. So why can't we be those people who can let our daughters be born and live so that they, too, can make us a proud parent one day?

The time has come when the people of this nation must rise together to protect their daughters. Destroy those who dare destroy our daughters!

Widows: Victims of Age Old Traditions

Widow. The word consumes itself.
—Sylvia Plath

A widow is a widow is a widow. Lifeless, sorrowful, helpless and eternally doomed. Well, that's what life is for a woman when she becomes a widow.

The man she was wedded to is no more, and though her husband may be physically dead, his wife is forced to lead a life of the living dead. She becomes a nonentity and her existence a journey filled with thorns. This may sound strange, but even in India today, we treat widows with scorn as was the practice in the past. So much so that it often makes me question if we as a nation have even progressed? Do we still feel smothered by the weight of our traditional culture?

There are more than forty million widows in India and for the majority of them, life is what some have described as a 'living sati', a reference to the now outlawed practice of widow burning. Only 28 per cent are eligible for pensions, and of that number, less than 11 per cent actually receive the payments to which they're entitled. If a woman is not financially independent, she's at the mercy of her in-laws, her parents and her family.

Being a widow in India is a taboo. People treat them as outcasts and untouchables. They are ostracized by society and kept away from social circles. They are barred from celebrating any festivals, rituals or joyous occasions and are forced to think of themselves as nothing but a burden on others. The inhuman treatment is heart wrenching.

It is not as if a woman's identity comes only from her husband. She is as much an individual as you and me. The disparity between a man and woman's status becomes clear here. A widower is not treated with scorn, but life becomes a living hell for woman who's husband dies. She is often held responsible for the tragedy and branded manhoos (jinxed) and inauspicious—as if any woman would pray for such miseries to fall upon her. While a man has the options to remarry, the woman is forced to live a life of penance as a punishment for what has transpired.

A visit to the holy city of Benaras will open your eyes to the unjust treatment of widows. Shunned and abandonded by their families, hundreds and thousands of widows live there in ashrams hoping to find some peace and solace. Some beg to earn money to sustain themselves.

Traditionally, Bengal has been particularly harsh in its treatment of widows. The centuries-old tradition of child marriage also prevailed in that region, in accordance with the myth that the god Siva took Parvati as his wife when she was only eight years old. As Hindu India was a polygamous society, a man could have several wives, and often the girls were married off to much older men. There was even a tradition of giving daughters in marriage to travelling Brahmin priests who would come to visit a family for a night, marry the daughter, before moving on and leaving her behind.

Girls married off as children stayed in their parents' homes until puberty and only then could the husband come to claim them. Unsurprisingly, these girls were often widowed and though they were still children, the restrictions applied. The miserable life they were forced to lead even at the tender age of ten or eleven made them lose hope, will and vitality.

The new age woman, as powerful and dynamic as men, is now a global phenonmena, but here in India we are still confined to our archaic traditions. When women are competing successfully with and overtaking their male colleagues in business, are we doing justice by branding women as widows and taking away their basic right to live with dignity? And yet we talk about women's liberation and rights. Are we promoting double standards of sorts? Ironically, the most powerful woman in India, Sonia Gandhi, is a widow too, so if we can accept her as a person capable of running our nation why can't we let other widows decide how they want to live their lives?

Even though there are several NGOs and other organizations working with the government to change the atititude towards widows in small states and towns of India, they have not succeeded greatly. This is mainly because of people's rigid views and notions and concern about the reaction within their immediate society or the neighbourhood. Community backlash is the greatest impediment people fear and because of this they are reluctant to change.

Education through films, street performances, road shows, interactive sessions, radio programmes and television shows can work wonders and also reach a wider audience. Roping in film and television personalities to talk about such issues will also help as people in smaller towns idolize actors and entertainers. It is important that the subject of widow rehabilitation be sensitively explained to families so that they understand that these women are as much human as any other member. Curbing their desires is no way to treat them. They, too, deserve a life beyond their dead husbands and so should be given a chance to live a happy life.

The government should organize rehabilitation camps and train widows on ways to earn a sustainable livelihood so that they become self-sufficient and independent. Relying on their husbands' families makes them even more miserable. If they can work and earn their own living it will give them a sense of confidence and the strength that they, too, can achieve something in life. They deserve as much respect as anyone else and so instead of sympathizing with them, connect with them and give them the courage to discover their potential.

The silver lining is that people everywhere, especially the cities, are acknowledging the importance of widow remarriage, and we should do everything possible to encourage the trend.

The Two Lives of a Politician

Sincerity should form the base of a true leader's life. Anyone who forgets this maxim is sure to be thrown down from his throne.

Though democracy is all about people (of the people, by the people and for the people), unfortunately in certain situations people come last. Take for example our politicians who are first to talk about the people and are last to serve them. They believe in just self-service and are not shy in being otherwise. Interestingly, as you will observe, it is their dual policies that make them symbols of double standards. Talk about one thing and do something else. Even if you come across a honest person you will tend to question his integrity and intentions.

In public, a politician is all smiles. Dressed in simple khadi, he stands with folded hands and talks about matters which concern the poor almost as if he can find a solution to their problems then and there. He is humble and understanding and will mingle with the public as if his purpose is to connect with them and understand their problems first hand. This is the public face of a politician.

Now, turning to the very private life of this very humble and down-to-earth politician.

He wears a costly Italian suit to go with his designer shoes.

He or she has an extensive wardrobe, the best jewellery, gold-rimmed goggles, the costliest cars, swanky flats and what not.

He dines at five-star hotels, moves about in big flashy cars, attends the biggest of the parties with the richest of industrialists and other celebrities, uses his many relatives' names to run businesses and makes investments in dozen of benami houses.

But in public he criticizes the same people whose parties he has just attended and sheds tears for the poor, talks about corruption and blames everyone around, except, of course, himself. On one hand, he talks about increasing corruption, crime, rape and murder and the urgent need to fight them, and on the other, he himself happily indulges in the same crimes.

And the irony is, the politician goes on dong this without any fear ... day after day, month after month, year after year.

It is as if he knows this is the right way to fool people and rule over them. However, I must admit that we have had some great politicians, but the tragedy is that they are the endangered species and the double-faced political animals are everywhere to be seen.

Now what will all this lead to?

The country's politicians are mostly an unsavoury lot. Of the 522 members of Parliament, 120 of them would be facing criminal charges, around 40 of them are accused of serious crimes, including murders and rape. Most Indian politicians are presumed to be corrupt, which is not at all surprising. No wonder, Indian politics has become much muckier in the recent years.

After getting elected to positions of power, most politicians ignore the reality and believe in the power of hoodwinking the public. They say anything that suits them, regardless of logic. By promising heaven to everyone, they make the political atmosphere a hell.

Free food, free loans, free land, free oil or whatever they like, becomes their motto till the time votes do not fall in their kitty. To fool people they can go to any length.

If everything will be given free or for less, then where will the money come from? Again these are the same old tricks. Ask the centre to give thousands of crores of rupees, and if it's not received, just blame the centre and strengthen further the concept of regional parties and continue to fool and rule. Imagine, if every state develops a regional party that behaves like that, what will happen to the nation?

This regional drama must stop, instead a constructive national thinking should prevail to keep India and all her citizens in good, improved conditions.

Only those politicians should join government, whether at the centre or state or municipality or panchayat, who practise the karma of a 'Monk'.

Are We a Nation of Fictitious Values and Double Standards?

By abandoning the genuine values of life, we only fall into a number of unforeseen entanglements. It is only by walking on the path of truth, do we get nearer to life.

There is a flash of smile on his face, but he is not smiling.

His eyes are filled with tears, but he is not crying.

Someone says 'yes', but deep within he really wants to say 'no'.

Gone are the days when you could gauge the truth from a person's facial expression. Sadly, it has become really difficult to know if a person's emotion is genuine or not.

If you analyse any relationship, you will be baffled. A husband prefers to be called pati parmeswar even if he is a cheat, a philanderer, a tyrant or a bully. Similarly, wives like to be defined as pativrata even if they have no real love, dedication or commitment towards their husbands. Is it not a charade how people would like to be addressed in public?

No relationship today is devoid of such fakeness, be it between a father and son, lovers, siblings or friends. Frankly, the concept of 'genuine love' is hard to come by or to say it ruthlessly, it is almost dead. If we fabricate so many emotions in our daily relationships, what is the need to maintain them? If we want relationships to be so superficial and shallow, why not detach ourselves from them?

A son calls his mother up and exchanges pleasantries, filling her heart with words of comfort when, deep down, he knows that it is only part of his weekly duties as a son and that most of his words are meaningless and are a ploy to get more financial favours from her. A daughter-in-law speaks well about her in laws in public even though she dislikes them, but she has to because 'kehana padta hai'. Work relationships, too, have not escaped such phony emotions. A junior hates his boss, but has to praise him to keep his/her job secure. Two colleagues might not get along but have to do so to maintain team spirit and work. The world around us is full of such bogus cases of love and friendship.

It is important to turn such superfluous relationships into something real because they end more quickly than they are formed. When the truth surfaces, they tend to harm our notions about what is good and bad, right and wrong.

In our immediate lives we can still exercise control over those who we want to befriend or trust, but we are often helpless when we deal with the world outside our realm, like in the case of the politicians. Day after day, year after year, politicians make promises, few of which are fulfilled while others lead to new ones. The cycle goes on and on. They continue to loot the nation of her wealth and resources under the guise of fake promises when their real motive is power. Standing on the podium they promise the poor money, jobs, better standards of living and much more, but once they descend from the platform, they start strategizing on how to manipulate the situation in their favour and make fools of those who trusted them and voted for them. How double faced these people are. They may condemn poverty in the country, but are the biggest reasons for it. They may pontificate on malnutrition and people starving to death, but have no qualms about holding back food grains and letting them rot in warehouses rather than distributing them for free among the impoverished. If you ask them if they have ever actually thought about the deprived sections of society or considered forsaking their interests to help them, the answer will be a shameless no.

Everyone denounces corruption, but almost everyone is corrupt. Many praise democracy, but their conduct is dictatorial. The person who talks about efficiency turns out to be the most inefficient. The one who professes honesty proves to be a real example of dishonesty. The sadhu in the garb of a godman is in reality no better than a criminal. Indeed, the world today is a breeding ground for such hypocritical people.

Would it be incorrect to say that we are a nation of liars? Whether intentional or or not we have all at some point in our lives faked emotions and feelings. Be it towards our close friends or relatives or those who we claim to admire and respect. If we look deep within ourselves, we will come across many such examples. So why blame others when we are equally at fault?

The nation may be full of dubious politicians but we are the ones who are responsible for bringing them to power. When we exercise our right to vote, do we actually research the antecedents of our candidate? Do we vote for him because he has done a good job in the past or because he belongs to a certain political family? Double standards, hypocrisy, artificiality have become a norm today.

Have you ever wondered why other countries do not take us seriously as a nation? Why there are so many examples that brand us as soft, casual, flippant and insincere? Perhaps the world is aware of our weaknesses and the tendency to change directions and positions. Such revelations hurt, but these are the fundamental realities that harm our image.

Has being artificial become our national identity? Let us ponder over this thought.

Being superficial has no long-term benefits. Forming artificial relationships can only bring you close to like-minded people, while distancing yourself from reality and can make you happy for a while but will ultimately lead to heartbreak, pain and suffering. Fake relations damage careers, life and the future and can be devastating on a personal level it. At a national level, however, it can have an adverse effect on our relationships with our neighbouring countries, and can lead to economical, political and social turmoil and isolation.

No country wants to be recognized as a country of shallow people; nothing can be worse than such a reputation. So are we an unhappy nation? I am never surprised when I hear 'complaints' about the nation and its state of affairs. These are not ordinary complaints but have far deeper roots that can have an extraordinary impact on our lives and the future. Therefore, it is all the more important for each individual and the nation to take note of this artificiality and double standards. We should all think about the 'realities' and our tendency to exist in a denial mode.

But what exactly are the reasons for this all pervading artificiality and fakeness? I think the cause perhaps lies in our 'cultural conditioning' arising from the rift between our strong and restrictive cultural traditions and the energy, quest, passion and fight for personal freedom, especially among the younger generation. Caught between these two we are confused about what to follow and what not to.

It is as if we tend to take the easy way out rather than do what is 'not desired' in any relationship. Play the double game that suits both parties. It could be the fear of losing grip of the relationship or protecting it forever, or it could be because of being over possessive. It could also be about being too conscious of a 'public image' and trying to preserve and protect it at any costs. However, what we don't realize is that by seeking a temporary 'social harmony', we are creating personal disharmony by constantly adjusting and fantasizing in every aspect of the relationship and life.

It appears as if we are not being mature enough to call a spade a spade and, at the same time, cultivate and nurture a great relationship based on truth, understanding and mutual harmony.

It is as if we are not being truthful and rational to ourselves or to our lives. But can anyone ever avoid or ignore truth for long? Can a life of lies and deceit ever provide any real satisfaction?

The time has come to accept the truth as truth and be mature and wise enough to understand it, analyse it and find harmonious ways to live with it rather than making a habit of suppressing it, hiding it and living a life of constant lies. The time has come to stop living a life with fictitious values and start living a life with genuine ones.

Because when it is real it is life.

We Want Justice!

It's all over now. Damini is dead. But she has left behind a profound vacuum, an abysmal darkness and a volley of some harrowing and brutal questions for a male-dominated society to answer. Instead of ignoring them, we must face them honestly. Although we are engulfed by feelings of confusion and hopelessness, we must put them aside and make efforts to find a more positive and conducive environment for women.

The brutal gang rape and murder of the young medical student in a moving bus in Delhi shocked the entire nation. As the news of her death was released the entire nation and especially the youth came out in hoards to demand justice for the innocent girl. There was a national uproar and demand for death penalty for the culprits. The entire nation stood together and grieved for the girl and also showed a sense of solidarity towards her plight, as it could have been just any girl that day. But the citizens' pleas seem to have fallen upon deaf ears because instead of action being taken against those who failed to do their duty, all we saw was chaos and confusion and the real cause was lost in the resulting bedlam.

The entire incident seems to have distintegrated into a tragic tale of hope and failed promises. The big question is do we have a right to demand justice even if injustice is being meted out in full public view and knowledge? Will our shout for 'WE WANT JUSTICE' ever lead to anything fruitful? Is our system so crippled that it cannot differentiate between right and wrong, or is it so full of lapses and inherent contradictions that to expect justice is asking for too much?

Let us get into a 'situation room' and analyse where the problem lies and whom to blame. Is it us, our social setup, our mental makeup or cultural conditioning? Looking at the changing realities and equations between men and women in modern India can also prove beneficial in reaching some conclusion.

Let's face it. Today's women are a different lot; they are far more independent, empowered and capable. As a result their demand for gender equality in all spheres is increasing. As more opportunities for women open up they are fast proving to be equal or even more capable than men. Science, technology, art, commence, administration, police, aviation, healthcare, social work, politics…you name the field and they are emerging at the top. So, logically, they should not be treated as the weaker sex anymore but as an equal and strong one.

Women today are bold, expressive and very much aware of the world around them. The new age woman is confident and sophisticated. They dress, talk, and think freely and are no longer hesitant to air their views. They enjoy going to pubs and bar and partying in public places just like their male counterparts. But, what is tragic is that, even in this day and age, some conservative and regressive men find it hard to accept their new-found independent status. These self-proclaimed moral policemen consider it their duty to enforce limits on women and teach them a lesson if they flounder and break rules. For example, the Bengaluru pub incident or the Guwahati incident where a group of rowdy men attacked a lone woman, tore her clothes off and assaulted her dignity, all because she was out drinking in the company of a male friend. Who gave them the right to think on behalf of the girl on what was right or wrong or how she should conduct herself in public? If anyone deserved to be punished then it should have been these men for harbouring such sick thoughts.

The Delhi rape incident is not a stray example of the barbaric methods men use to rob women of their dignity. History is full of many such examples, but only few make headline news while others fall into oblivion or are not reported. The fact remains that men continue to unleash atrocities on women, yet there is little that our government and the law are doing to stop this.

After the Delhi rape case, even though every citizen joined together to show anger and frustration towards the system and the repeated failure of government to improve the situation, somewhere along the line the core issue became diluted and the main demand sidelined. During one of the processions at Raisina Hill, a policeman was killed and the entire focus shifted from the talk of justice to the mystery surrounding his death. This started the blame game, confusion, accusations and counter accusations. Police had one version; the doctors a different opinion while eye-witnesses had another story. While media took up the baton to solve his death, in the entire melee the common man and his cause was abandoned.

While Delhi's chief minister and the country's prime minister were struggling to move into damage control mode, the entire nation had lost hope. After all, this did not concern just one girl, but all girls who feel insecure whether they live in cities or rural areas. It is about their right to live a fearless life. If no government or law can offer them the security they seek, then they have absolutely no right to stay in power. Blaming Western culture or women's attire or their boldness to act and be equal to men has got nothing to do with the rise in crime against women because if that was true then rapes would never take place in rural areas. It has everything to do with the kind of mentality people possess, and if there is anything that needs to undergo drastic change then it is the psyche and mental make-up of people at large.

On one hand, we talk about women power and giving the girl

child the right she deserves, and on the other, we are a country with highest number of female foeticide cases. It just goes to prove that we are a nation of contradictions. We tend to support some women's causes, but continue to deny them their basic rights. We desperately need to change our attitudes, not by preaching and teaching but by practicing what we offer as solutions to others. Mere talking will not work anymore, we need to take immediate actions to salvage the situation.

There is a strong demand to increase police presence everywhere. But will this be possible? Why do we need police to guard our thinking? Can we not change our attitude towards women on our own? And what can the police do when it has been observed that in over 40 per cent of rape cases the tormentor is a friend, relative or a known person. People have also lost faith in the law and policemen are least trusted. Families and women prefer not to go to police stations in case they are harassed by the personnel, or they are nervous that they will be forced to provide graphic details of the horrific incident. The insensitivity of the police personnel is one of the biggest reasons why justice is delayed or denied to the victim.

Tackling the problem at the grassroots level can lead to a positive change to a great extent. First and foremost, the need is to sensitize our police forces. They should be trained on how to treat the victim or the complainant; the aim should be to first give them proper counselling and immediate first aid rather than insisting on getting the details of their experiences.

Another step, specific to our cities, could be to increase police vigilance at night and the presence of female personnel in police stations at all hours, especially in crime prone areas. If the government can provide security cover to ex-ministers and army chiefs then why can't they do the same for common citizens? Even though there is a stringent demand for the death penalty for those accused of rape, the punishment should depend upon the facts of the case. Punishments like chemical castration and life imprisonment can act as stronger deterrents.

So can a change in law bring about the necessary changes in people's minds and their lives? There are two ways to approach the problem: one is the fear of law and the other sensitization and proper education.

Part of the problem is we are two distinctive cultures—maybe even two countries—in one country: the 'modern' India as well as 'traditional' Bharat. Serious efforts should be made to sensitize all those who are in a position of power to view the new woman in the right perspective. Our society needs to understand and reconcile with the changes and recast its attitudes accordingly. This is the real fight.

It is rightly observed that there can be no real development in today's India without the participation of our youth and most importantly of women. And if we believe that woman's emancipation and independence leads to real empowerment, we should recognize their values and work towards their betterment. Only this will give the nation the inspiration and cause for celebration.

Part 2

Confessions of a Romantic

My soulmate has been perfect for me. We have lived together for thirty years. I don't have any complaints against her... nothing exists for me beyond her...without her. She has a perfection of a kind...

She is an enigma for me as well as for others. She has a protean personality. She is a very senior bureaucrat. In her professional life she is a very honest, but tough person. Her evaluation of plans and possibilities is of the highest quality. Her sense of justice and moral uprightness define her character. A combination of ice and steel makes her a formidable boss.

But, she is a complete contrast at home. Here she is the typical, traditional Indian housewife. Her devotion to her uxorial duties boggles my mind all the time. All her activities have absolute finesse. She always wears authentic Indian clothes. And yet, she wields a quiet authority. For my parents she has been the ideal bahu.

Living with a woman under the same roof is not a simple task. It's probably the most complex situation. The hold of a domestic spring is the most difficult thing to escape from. Like all dutiful and ideal husbands, I too accept my domestic obligations and bonds with the utmost alacrity. It shocks all those who are in favour of freedom.

This is the most opportune moment to confess to everyone that this matrimonial alliance has given me the greatest pleasure. The high quality of my married life must be a source of envy for all those acquaintances whose marriages have been a constant battleground. Any husband forced to live with a shrew knows well how life turns into virtual hell if one's life partner is unsympathetic and lacks understanding. Here too I'm the luckiest guy. She is a paragon of feminine qualities. I do fall short in coming up to her expectations, but she has not done so in mine. She has been a flawless daughter-in-law, a caring mother and everything else.

Over the years she has nurtured all her relationships with unquestionable skill. All my family members have experienced happiness in her company. Her inherent charisma has won them all over. And if they forced into rejecting one of us, I'm sure it will be me.

The citadel she has enclosed our family within is warm and secure and notwithstanding my best efforts, I haven't found even a smallest chink in it. As husband I don't have, shouldn't have any complaints against her. In the eyes of others and in my eyes too, she is the embodiment of femininity. Her mind is beautiful and her soul, pious.

I'll be worst the husband if I criticize her in any way. Yet, I must share my secret grudge against her today. I'm an incorrigible romantic. I want my beloved wife to openly, boldly and fearlessly, call me by my intimate name. My ears have been longing for that. But she is adamant about this. Before others, she addresses me as 'Suno ji.'

My heart pains at that…but not for a moment do I doubt her immense love for and devotion towards me. I have understood well that she is a true daughter of the great Indian tradition. The one who has defined the true meaning of the husband—wife relationship. The one that has been passed down to her from her mother, grandmother, great-grandmother and so on…. In spite of her high status in society, she would never forget her cultural heritage.

My romantic proclivity has made me a better person. Now my heart goes out to all those who have been suffering in any way. This has also made me love my life and the world that I live in. Love has become the essence of my being. And, whom do I owe it to? You guess it!

Change with Continuity

Acceptance of change is the beginning of wisdom.

Nothing is permanent than change. Life changes, so do lifestyles. Change happens the way we dream, aspire, think, behave or how we develop our outlooks, attitudes, conduct or behaviour. We call the change by different names: transformation, evolution, generational shifts, new age thinking and lifestyles and so on and so forth. If you take a close look at the ever-changing life, you will discover that evolution is all about continuity and change coexisting simultaneously.

And that is a good thing to happen for society and the other social units to experience more harmony and less friction.

For example, think of a pattern of behaviour. Years ago in our country, according to our tradition and culture, whenever we would meet a senior, we greeted him/her by touching his/her feet. This changed to just a namaskar, then came the handshake and now is the time to hug and kiss or just to casualy ask how you are.

On closer observation, you will notice that all these changes are happening in a steady, evolving, continuous way, I mean a step-by-step change...not sudden, like moving from touching the feet to a kiss on the cheek.

A sudden change may not be proper because it may be hard to digest. Thus, in every sphere, changes occur with a constant flow of continuity and change. And in this manner, everything changes conforming to the norms of social harmony. Take for example the pattern in which we dress. Before, it was mostly sarees and dhotis, kurtas, then came shirts and trousers, then shorts or even bikinis...

But the bikinis never happened straight from ghunghat lest there should be complete disconnect and disharmony. Like this in almost all spheres, the clothes we wear, the food we eat, the music we listen to, the plays or cinema we see, or for that matter the way we think and behave... everything has to be a reflection of continuity and change, not a sudden disconnect. All of civilization is going through the pattern of change.

But the problem is, some of our youth, being euphoric and obsessed with the changed world, especially those influenced by the West and its thrust on absolute individualism, care little about our cultural heritage and traditional values. They take them for granted and start thinking and behaving in a manner that is completely disconnected from our values. Such behaviour may hurt sentiments and cause pain and anguish, thus youngsters should avoid indulging in habits that are not acceptable. So the best way would be to welcome change, but with some reservation.

No one wants to live in the fifteenth century today. No, not at all. The need of the hour is that the new should remain connected with the old, if not with the oldest. It is essential to keep the old and adopt the new so that life moves on with harmony.

Traditional Indian Gestures and their Inherent Godliness

Namaste and touching the feet of elders are traditional Indian ways of greeting. By following them, we keep our cultural identity alive. Not only that—this small gesture of respect is a great symbol of our heritage.

Namaste.

The moment you arrive in India, the first words you will probably hear are 'namaste' or 'namaskar', which are both informal or formal ways of greeting. They can be used either as a welcome or when saying goodbye. Namaste is also a part of Southeast Asian cultures and is now a globally accepted form of greeting.

The word is a combination of the Sanskrit namah (to bow) and te (you), and means I bow to you. It has a deeper spiritual significance of reducing a person's ego in the presence of others. It is also believed that Namaste denotes that the divinity and god that lives within us is the same. In other words, the god spirit in one person recognizes and honours the god spirit in another.

Namaste is usually accompanied by a slight bow made with both palms pressed together with the fingers pointed upwards. Even without saying the word, the gesture conveys the same meaning. Also known as Anjali Mudra (or Pranamasana), it is a pan Indian gesture that is used when greeting gods, family, siblings, friends, strangers, irrespective of age, gender or social status. Occasionally, however, it varies according to prestige or status. For example, namaste is a sign of respect when a person from a lower social status greets one whose status is higher.

An incident from the ancient Hindu epic, the Mahabharata, explains how namaste can also be used to appease a person. When Lord Krishna stole the clothes of the young gopis while they were bathing in the Yamuna, they were scared that they would have to return home naked and fervently pleaded with him to return their garments. But he continued to tease them with his pranks and it was only after they bowed before him, with folded hands, that he responded to their urgent requests.

Namaste, as a gesture, can be used in various ways. The traditional way suffices when greeting friends or peers, but for an older person, the palms are pressed in front of the forehead, as a mark of respect. When worshipping a god or another deity, the palms are generally placed above the head, with the head bowed and eyes shut.

When two people greet each other, it signifies 'may our minds meet'. The act of bowing one's head is a gracious form of showing love, respect and humility towards others. At times, namaste is accompanied by intoning the names of gods like 'Jai Sri Krishna', 'Ram, Ram', 'Hari Om', either at the beginning of a conversation or at its end. Often, even a written communication ends with these words, instead of best wishes, sincerely, regards and such like.

Sadly, today, this traditional form of greeting is considered 'uncool' by the upwardly mobile.

Touching feet: A symbol of receiving an elder's love and blessings

India, like every other country, has her own culture, traditions and customs that are deeply rooted in the history and ethos of the land. Although we are still proud of our heritage, many of us are unaware of its subtle nuances.

Often, people are mystified when they see a child touching

the feet of an elder. Yet, this is one of our most common gestures signifying respect and submission towards those who are superior to us in both age and position. It is one of the earliest lessons in manners and etiquette taught to Indian children, who are expected to touch the feet of their parents and elders, who in turn respond by placing their right hands on the children's heads, blessing them with long life, fortune and success.

Touching the feet of both gods or elders symbolizes shraddha (devotion) and karuna (compassion). Its origin dates back to Satyayuga, when devotees used to touch the feet of Lord Vishnu. Later, people began to touch the feet of rishis and gurus because they were revered as the incarnations of god. Today, however, parents are regarded as gurus, which is why this act is first extended to them and then to the other elders.

There are several other occasions when this gesture is considered auspicious as well, indicative of a person's deep respect for god and nature's bounty, for example, on festivals and religious events, during weddings and even when departing for or returning from a journey.

However, there is some logic behind this tradition. According to modern science, the human body contains positive and negative currents of electricity—the left side carries the negative current while the right carries the positive. When the two halves meet they form a complete circuit of positive and negative chakras. Touching the feet acts like a light being switched on allowing a current to flow from the elder towards the one performing the salutation, setting in motion the transfer of good health, success, fortune and happiness.

If you would like your child to touch your feet every morning, develop this habit from a very young age so that this tradition is deeply ingrained and becomes part of life. If this is so, he will not be embarrassed if he performs it in public.

We bemoan the fact that our traditional values have declined today, but if we want future generations to accept them, we must make them understand the power and godliness behind our customs.

It is important to make our youth aware of the significance of such gestures.

The Son of God as the Sun God

If I had to choose a religion, the sun as the universal giver of life would be my God.
—Napoleon Bonaparte

The sun is the source of radiance in our lives since it protects us from all evil. Throughout human history, the Sun God has been worshipped by different names in different civilizations. It is revered both as a celestial body and the giver of life, and is hailed as the most potent giver of the spirit. Worshipping the sun is regarded as being close to the ultimate force in the universe that in turn will help us connect with divinity.

How we live makes us who we are. If we examine our traditions or take a look at our ancient sculptures, we will discover how our great rishis and munis emphasized the benefits of healthy living. Inculcating those habits will help us lead radiant, healthy, energetic and positive lives. Unfortunately, the influence of Western culture has made us ignore our traditional ways of living.

One step towards building a healthy lifestyle is to perform the surya namaskar every morning. It is the best way to kick-start your day and help your quest for a stress-free life. But to benefit from its asanas (postures), it is essential to understand its importance, as well as the sun's significance in our lives.

Imagine a world without the sun. There will be darkness

all around with no source of light. It would mean the end of existence for all creatures that thrive in sunlight. Without the sun, the entire cosmic system will collapse. Now think of the sun's life preserving and nurturing qualities, and how it inspires positive and peaceful thoughts. Its aura encompasses you wherever you are, and like a true friend, guide and philosopher it keeps you company at all times.

Yes, the sun is everywhere and there can be no darkness when the sun is spreading its light. Even the evil karmas of human nature cannot remain hidden from its brightness. At the same time, it also destroys all malevolent and sinful thoughts and desires.

To pray or to bow before the sun is equal to worshipping god. Like him the sun is omnipresent and represents life and good health. No wonder our great sages discovered the power of the sun and recommended the value of the surya namaskar in our daily life.

The key to an effective surya namaskar is to prastice it in its entirety with all its mantras and postures. It can also be performed as a physical exercises or complete sadhana, which incorporates body positions, breathing exercises and profound medication. Follow it regularly to keep your body fit and your mind and soul peaceful.

In today's highly charged, stressful world it is essential to adhere to a strict physical regime, whether at home or in a gym. If you can, try to squeeze in some time for the surya namaskar. If you can't, salute the Sun God by offering him water every morning instead. According to Hindu tradition, this is also a form of worship that devotees follow with great fervour. Add some rose or other flower petals to the water and offer that to the morning sun. Try it. I can assure you that your life will be transformed.

To Love or Not to Love

Love looks not with the eyes, but with the body.
—William Shakespeare

It is said that love is the best lover in the world.
Love is hope. Love is light, but it just has to be right! Surely this is a positive attitude that brings hope, joy and happiness to one's life.

In life we come across different kinds of love. Some of the purest forms of love are that between a mother and child, siblings, friends, god and devotee, towards animals and other forms of natural life. But different people view love differently.

The male and female perception of love usually differs and can be termed the ying and yang or gender-based understanding of love. Although the exact definition of love is unconditional care, sharing and trust, for a man it is more like a facile, superficial experience that involves sex, beauty and other physical attributes. A woman, on the other hand, connects love with deeper feelings of trust, compatibility, understanding and passion.

The young today are confused and often label love as lust, even though the two are as different as chalk and cheese. But what the young fail to understand is that relationships based on lust and sex falter as quickly as they are forged. For love to be everlasting, it should be pure and free from social pressures or any other types of external influences.

There is no denying that sex is very much part of love, but

it only becomes meaningful, when there is a genuine emotion attached to it. It then blossoms into a rare bonding that fulfills the craving for physical intimacy.

The question now is: how can a man and a woman ensure a relationship based on true love if both their views differ so drastically?

The answer is simple: by displaying the emotions that are essential to keeping the relationship alive.

If there is an emotional attachment, then naturally one becomes more caring to the other's needs, desires, dreams and aspirations. And if love is mutual then there is every possibility that each will go that extra mile to maintain a joyful relationship. A successful relationship is one where both are partners in joy as well as sorrow, through good times and bad. But when a relationship sours, then the only outcome can be sad and bad, which leads to further misunderstandings that can make the lovers bitter, negative and miserable about each other. So much so that both lose hope in love.

When a person discovers that his/her partner is involved in an extra marital affair, he/she feels cheated and betrayed and there is a final breach of trust when the relationship ends. People who have gone through such a devastating experience find it hard to trust another person and accept love for fear of being left heartbroken again.

Why do people create such bad vibes in a loving relationship?

Why not be more caring and build a relationship that is enduring?

The crux of the matter lies in respecting the sanctity of love and to only pursue a relationship if you are really sure of approaching it in the right way. It is only then that life becomes more positive and ultimately reflects in your behaviour, mannerisms and attitude.

Love will certainly make life more fulfilling. I read this

somewhere that love has also a quality of silence. It conspires with the secret thoughts of two lovers. Brings them much closer in their physical absence. A lover is a sacred poet, the kindest and the most generous soul on earth. Only he can see through the entanglements of the diurnal existence. It endlessly drives him to give out his best of the world. It imports to him a faith in beauty. He can destroy hostility, selfishness and all other morbidities. Love can generate a purifying force and redeem humanity from imminent destruction.

So keep spreading love!

Love Thy Servants

A good servant is a real godsend, but truly this is a rare bird in the hand.

—*Martin Luther*

By being a little more considerate towards those who serve us, we can ensure their everlasting loyalty and happiness.

Do you know anything more about your driver other than the time he arrives in the morning and leaves in the evening?

The chances are an empathic no!

Do you know when your maidservant feels hungry?

Again, naturally, the answer will be no, or why the heck should I bother?

Yes, therein lies the problem.

It is very unfortunate that we have little concern for the people who are an integral part of our daily life, and who serve us with dedication. These are the same people without whom our lives will come crumbling down if they are not around for even a day.

Think of your driver. Try to realize what he gives and what he gets in return. This is the man who is at your command whenever you want him. He takes extra effort to ensure that your ride is comfortable and safe and that you reach your destination on time. Be it summer, winter, or a rainy day, he appears at your doorstep without fail, at the designated time. When he willingly drives you to a friend's office or residence in the scorching heat, do you ever bother to enquire if he has eaten or drunk water to quench his thirst? Never. But the question is: why don't you care? He is ever the loyal servant, privy to all confidential matters. While in the car, you discuss business deals and plans, your personal life, gossip about colleagues and friends. He is witness to your extra marital affairs or other clandestine activities. But, true to his spirit of loyalty, he seldom divulges what he sees or hears to the outside world. Neither does he charge you extra for favours done.

When he greets you with a smile and big salute first thing in the morning you feel like a maharaja.

Have you ever thought what these special gestures mean? And what do these people get in return?

A rebuke, a frown, the threat of losing their jobs. A single mistake, like being late for work, taking an extra day off or inadvertently denting the car—any one of these could mean the end of his job.

Have you ever mulled over this? Have you ever thought about how your ill temper can impact upon the people who serve you so tirelessly day and night?

Is it justified? Think about it and you will realize what I mean.

Is it our arrogance or their poverty and dependency that make us so indifferent that we often forget that they are human beings too. Even they have feelings and needs that they want to achieve through sheer hard work.

Think and you will certainly find the answers.

Sadly, if someone does anything that is contrary to our liking, we lose all sense of proportion and refuse to accept the other's point of view.

We get so furious about trivial matters that we forget the loyalty and sincerity of those who serve us.

If the same maid, who attends to our needs everyday, makes a little mistake, she is severely upbraided and threatened that she will lose her job.

And if the same driver who has served us so loyally makes

a small mistake like arriving late for duty, he has to bear the brunt of your anger.

Why can't we think of them as human beings and treat them in the same way we do towards family and friends?

We have forgotten all the lessons we have learnt from our ancient scriptures and the teachings of our wise rishis and munis. Our culture is humane and values brotherhood, kindness and compassion. It has never taught us to behave in such an uncouth manner.

This story is an example of our changing attitudes: A poor but compassionate Brahmin from the hills brought up his orphaned nephew just like a son. He educated him and provided him with all that a child needs. The nephew later became a prominent officer and the Brahmin went to live with him. One day, he heard his nephew introduce him to a guest as his 'cook'. Confused, the old man wondered why he was not called kaka or uncle. When he realized the real meaning of the word, he left his nephew's house, heartbroken.

In the past, the servants of the house were treated like family members. Remember the ubiquitous 'Ramu kaka' and other faithful retainers who looked after us with care and love. Remember the stories they told us, the songs they sung.

Why don't we go back to those times and bring back those good habits again? In this way we will become more considerate and caring.

Why don't we make an attempt to know about our drivers, maids and other domestic help? Why don't we try to help them through the struggles of their lives?

Just help your driver educate his son, or find a good doctor for your maid's sick husband and see how they respond.

It is time we changed our attitudes to bring more smiles.

An Ode to a Mother

In a child's eyes, a mother is a goddess. She can be glorious or terrible, benevolent or filled with wrath, but she commands love either way. I am convinced that this is the greatest power in the universe.
—N.K. Jemisin

There is no greater feeling than that of motherhood. Nothing in the world can be better than motherhood. A mother is a creator. She has the power to heal the wounds of life. She is the ultimate symbol of universal love. She deserves her children's respect. By paying our obeisance to her we will certainly feel as if we have had the ultimate experience in life.

Everyone knows what a mother is. What it all takes to be a mother. And how valuable a mother is.

Human mother. Animal mother. Motherland. And Mother Earth.

Whichever way you think, the answer would probably be that there is simply no comparison to a mother.

Just imagine what a mother does. It may be yours or mine. Mothers all over the earth are unique.

Life giving, caring, eternally loving, sacrificing and always well-meaning….

True, it is the mother that attends to all our needs.

For mother, her child comes first. She does everything to nurture and nourish her baby till he/she grows up and is ready to walk alone.

Her mothering spirit never dies, come what may.

It only ends with her death.

How fortunate he/she is who has a mother!

One person, many roles. She is the best friend, philosopher and guide, and at times, plays the role of father, sister, brother and teacher too.

Nothing escapes her attention when it comes to the needs and aspirations of her child, whether expressed or not.

And nothing stops her from doing whatever it is to ensure that her children get what they want.

Who do you first think of when you face any problem? Naturally, mother.

Who do you fall back upon when in crisis? Naturally, mother.

We all understand this sacred fact of life.

Yes, in all the circumstances of life, our mother is the only person there by our side, always.

Because it is the mother who understands us and loves us unconditionally. Not sometimes, not once in a while but always and forever.

A mother promises security.

A mother is the best insurance against any hazards.

A mother is the eternal force that God has created to look up to, perhaps his greatest gift to mankind.

We salute the spirit of motherhood and bow before her with reverence! Thank you to all the mothers who are the embodiment of care.

My mother. Your mother. Motherland. And of course the Mother Earth.

Let us all say with pride, Mother you are the greatest!

The Everlasting Beauty of Sibling Bonds

A sibling is a friend given by nature.
— *Anonymous*

My brothers and sisters are my true strength. They are the ones who help me forever to get over the dark moments in life. Only through their association do I discover my own self. They always support me and keep me grounded. Our ties are sacred and we live for one another. 'I am my brother's keeper.'

The beauty of a relationship amongst brothers and sisters is better felt than described.

It's a very intimate relation that is lifelong. The genetic code, the blood link, the innate associations, the natural companionship and comradeship between siblings go a long way in enhancing the relationship further.

The understanding, the mutual trust and dependence between brothers and sisters come so naturally that each one discovers a little of his own self in the other. And this leads to a blind trust between them.

Have you ever felt the beauty of this relationship?

Well, in some cases, this relationship has been enriching, but unfortunately in others, the bond has been broken.

In today's 'me first' world, this splendid and sacred relationship has taken a back seat. Driven by selfish concerns, people do not maintain this special, lifelong bond. Still, when confronted by dire circumstances, the first persons we rush to for support are our blood relations or siblings. Then it becomes important to explore this multifaceted relationship. A sibling can be a friend, a confidant, a philosopher, and guide, and in rarest of cases, a father or mother figure. Only those who have been brought up with such strong familial relationships can understand their importance and what it means to have a sibling.

If appreciated, these priceless bonds can spice up life and introduce us to a multitude of emotions, which may otherwise not be discovered.

To say the least, it is only through these relationships that you will savour the many joys of life like trust, goodness, kindness, compassion, adventure, excitement, fun, sharing, caring, rearing and what not! So why not enjoy the relationship with your brother and sister and learn valuable lessons in love, compassion, trust and friendship through them.

The next time you think about life, think about your brothers and sisters and how much more beautiful and fulfilling it can be if shared with them.

I, too, have experienced great moments and memories with my dear brothers and sisters and I proudly nurture the relationship with great passion and fervour. I think if you do the same then you will discover much more love coming your way.

This relationship is most enviable, satisfying and beautiful. Trust it, love it and live with it every moment of your life!

Woh To Apke Baap Ke Bhi Baap Hai

My roots lie in you. I know that I cannot compensate for the love you bestowed upon me without any ulterior motive. Only you have taught me what love is.

Our country's greatest strength lies in the way in which we preserve our family bonds. The joint family system is unique to our culture and has also been internationally acknowledged as an example of how families should live. The unconditional bond of love that the various generations in a family share is remarkable. And what is even more remarkable is the heartwarming relationship between grandparents and their grandchildren.

Do you remember the time when your parents were busy with work? And your grandparents readily agreed to play with you in the way you wanted? They were the ones who always wanted to see you smiling and cheerful and were ready to do anything to ensure your happiness.

Have you ever thought about what they wanted in return for all the unconditional love and care that they bestowed upon you?

Nothing. Absolutely nothing.

Such is their great love for you.

Though grandparents had a very special place in our lives while we were growing up, the situation changed as we grew older and more involved with our lives. The same love and respect we had for them then were overshadowed by other concerns and priorities. As adults we need to understand that it is now our turn to return all the love, care and attention they so readily gave us. This will help us strengthen our relationships with them and bring happiness and peace to them in the lonely days of their lives.

Unfortunately, however, the youth of today have become selfish and are easily influenced by external influences. As a result they have conveniently forgotten their duties towards their grandparents who were so much a part of their growing-up years.

Think...

We at Paras Foundation run an old age home—Ghauranda—where we provide care to the aged who have been adandoned by their children and grandchildren. We provide them with decent accommodation, healthy and hygienic food, healthcare and many other facilities like a library and entertainment, absolutely free of cost. We believe that much more needs to be done for them, so that we can, as a symbolic gesture, give back what they did to enrich our lives.

Let us not think of the old as outdated and of no value. Let us not think of them as a burden to society. Let us not consider them as liabilities or a hindrance to our growth.

To think of them in such terms is wrong. Once we start to respect them, our lives will be brighter and richer.

They are the repositories of endless love, compassion, and above all, wisdom. When was the last time you discussed a new career plan with them or a business venture? When did you last buy them a gift? Or brought them some delicious snacks as a treat? When did you send them flowers? Or even a birthday card?

Perhaps never!

If you had done so, you would have seen a happy smile on their faces, or received their blessings. Do not let the routine, hectic pace of today's world diminish your bonds of love for your grandparents. Do not abandon this beautiful relationship because you are hard-pressed for time. Instead nurture it and let it grow, it will only make your life more meaningful.

Your Wife, your Life

She is there with you always. She is there for you till her last breath.

She never says never, and shares with you and cares for you, forever!

She is your wife, she is your partner for life.

Have you ever thought about what is so special about this woman, who leaves her former life and starts to build a new one by becoming your wife?

She leaves her father, mother, siblings and family to join yours till the end of her life.

Have you ever thought what this means?

What is remarkable is the level of her love, devotion and sacrifice, and above all, the determination to be with you always, whatever the circumstances, through joy and sorrow, sickness and health, good times and bad.

Imagine her sacrifice. She renounces personal interests and aspirations and adapts herself to your lifestyle and requirements.

Is not this woman truly special. And should she not be treated as such?

Does she not deserve something in return for all that she does for you?

Think deeply and her image will grow larger and larger.

Yes, your wife deserves much more love, care, respect and attention than what you think is necessary.

But, most of us tend to take our wives for granted.

We think that just because she's your wife, her duty is to

pander to the interests and needs of the family.

At times we upbraid her because it's our right. At times we may physically abuse her because, again, it's our right.

But, what we fail to understand is that she is a human being, an individual who wants an understanding and loving spouse. As a husband, it is the man's duty to take care of her needs and desires. He should be her closest friend and confidant.

The best gift a man receives is a child, but that is only courtesy his wife. The joys he experiences as a father is also made possible because of his wife. Childbirth is the most crucial time in a woman's life, but a husband will never understand the excruciating pain a woman goes through, unless he is by her side in the labour room. His presence will make the bond stronger and she will feel wanted and loved.

My advice is: start an affair with your wife.

Fall in love with her all over again.

It will elevate your relationship with her, as well as add spice to it.

It will enable you to discover a new her.

In turn it will reassure her that you are treating her as an individual and equal.

Respect her, woo her. Give her what she deserves and you will discover what she is capable of giving you in return. After all, in happiness and sorrow, she is the only person who will stand by your side. So start courting her again and see how your married life blooms.

Long Live the Father!

Father! Oh father! Oh father!
There is nothing like a father!
A father is awesome!
A father is playful!
A father is responsible!
A father is enthusiastic!
A father is strong!
Let every father live long!
Think about a father and his contribution to a child's life.

He is the hope. The guardian of destiny who works hard to preserve, protect and support his child's life.

He provides all needed security and confidence.

He shows the direction and helps fulfil all dreams.

Have you ever thought how valuable a father is to a child?

While a mother is the repository of unconditional love and compassion, a father is the provider of life and security.

A father is a benevolent disciplinarian who may not show his love openly, but goes out of the way to remove any thorns from the path his child treads.

This is the true idendity of the father who does everything possible to bring happiness to the life of his child and the family.

Who has always stood by your ambition and tried his best to help you achieve your goal?

Who toiled hard and with a burning zeal to ensure that you are secure?

Who has always guided you, taught you, shaped you so that

even after he is no more, you don't get caught by the challenges of life?

If the mother's emotions kept you alive in spirit, it is the father's reasoning that has shaped your life.

A father deserves all the love, respect and reverence for all that he does for his children.

He may not demonstrate his love or emotions, but his heart and mind is always tuned towards your welfare.

When it comes to emotions, we should not restrict ourselves to a particular day to tell our fathers how much we love them, care for them and respect them. Everyday should be a Father's Day so that we can celebrate the greatest hero in our lives.

With profound memories of all that my late father has done for me and for everyone in the family, I salute him. It is my humble request that each person rethink and rediscover the immense value of your father and the bond with him.

Because he is not just the giver of life, he preserves and protects it for you to live and enjoy it. The truth is when a father stands by his son, then the son is transformed into a warrior.

Life is not complete without a father.

A Wedding to Remember

The changing face of India has set the pace for many positive things. Trends that have become widely accepted are intercaste and crosscultural marriages. Indians go abroad to study or for better job prospects and often end up falling in love with people from different religions and cultures. But such minor hitches don't really matter when one is in love. Today, few eyebrows are raised if an Indian marries a foreigner, though some may still disapprove not realizing how important it is to keep pace with the changing times and its benefits to society.

Let me emphasize this point with an example where people gathered together to bless a couple who had met abroad and fallen in love despite their cultural and religious differences. Both families agreed to the match when they saw the deep love between the boy and girl. It was a simple love story but in this case, the girl came from an conservative and affluent Gujarati family and the boy from a free-thinking, liberal French lineage. Such scenarios are not unheard of in India, but for a girl from a conservative family to take such a drastic step is bold. But kudos to the girl's parents who happily accepted the decision of their daughter and even organized a wedding that symbolized the amalgamation of two very different cultures. Their acceptance displays the tolerance that new India possesses and the refreshing change in the attitudes of its people.

Kinjal, the daughter of my dear friend and India's well-known chemical, polymer and rubber trader, Pankaj Sayar, married a French boy called Benjamin. After much deliberation the girl finally accepted Bejamin's proposal and with it began the struggle to get the two families to accept their decision. It was only after the grandfather, Vitthal Das Laxmi Das Sayar, met the boy that the family agreed to the wedding.

The wedding took place with much fanfare in 2011, in Mumbai. The functions leading up to the wedding were planned in such a way that each event showcased the two cultures. The mehendi night was typically Indian and it was wonderful to see the foreign guests getting their palms painted with henna, swaying to the beats of Bollywood hits and enjoying Indian delicacies.

The next night, Pankaj Sayar hosted a cocktail and dinner party, where the theme was European. For this the décor was minimal yet elegant and cuisine distinctly French. In keeping with the theme, Kinjal's mother, Rajul, wore a stylish French gown. The camaraderie between the Indians and the French and the general merriment made this a truly mesmerizing evening.

The wedding ceremony on the third day was memorable and went off very smoothly with no awkward moments. What was particularly memorable was not the wealth on display, but how such a conservative family could happily and gracefully accept a family from another culture.

It is this type of broad-minded, modern thinking that makes us expand our knowledge as well as show tolerance towards another person's race, culture and tradition.

I felt truly inspired when I saw both families and their friends intermingle so harmoniously, sing songs, dance merrily to the tune of the bhangra and traditional Gujarati dandia and create an atmosphere of love, warmth and energy.

Communions like these should be eye-opener for all those who still believe and live in a caste and community ridden environment.

At last, the celebrations were over, leaving the guests with warm memories of the joyful event. As I was departing, I could almost hear everyone talking of the new India, the 'Badalte Bharat Ki Badalti Tasveer' (a changing portrait of a changing India)

I felt inspired by the changing image of my country, and how easily she can integrate with different cultures, faiths and religions. And the promises it carries to emerge from narrow-minded thoughts of caste, creed and religion.

Friendship is Forever

Don't walk in front of me,
I may not follow.
Don't walk behind me,
I may not lead.
Walk beside me and
Be my friend.

—Albert Camus

What a warm, democratic, friendly and a touching expression! Yes, that is the real meaning of a true friend. A friend is one who is always there with and for you. He is the one who knows everything about you and accepts your shortcomings and flaws. He is the one you can always depend upon when times are bad. He is your closest confidant, he keeps you well-grounded and protects you from false friends and flatterers. To have a friend in life is indeed one of the most precious relationships.

But is such a relationship becoming less important today? Are we living in an age where it is common to take advantage of our friends? Are our lives really filled with true friends?

Even though Friendship Day comes and goes, like any other day, do we really celebrate it in the spirit of what it signifies? Well it is difficult to comprehend what today's generation thinks, what their desires and aspirations are. The emotions and feelings that they demonstrate seem short-lived and fickle.

True friendship calls for sacrifices, selflessness, unconditional love, sharing and caring. Emotions, which are hard to come by these days. Yet there still are many who swear by this precious relation. History abounds with examples of true friendship. The bonds between Gertrude Stein and Ernest Hemmingway; Abraham Lincoln and Joshua Speed; women's rights activists Susan B. Anthony and Elizabeth Cady Stanton serve as the best examples of friends who have supported each other in their journey through life. Moreover, it cements the fact that everyone needs a friend.

Explaining the true meaning of a friend and friendship is difficult. It is indescribable as an emotion. One has to experience it to really know its real meaning. With time its meaning has changed, but the essence still remains. With every generation comes new definitions and meanings of the word. Maybe this generation of convenience, as I like to call it, does not give friendship much significance. For them friendship is related to selfish motives and using friends to their advantage. True, it's difficult to find examples of a deep and understanding friendship these days.

People have come to believe that a relationship that has its foundation in greed and self-interest is definitely not friendship. We must all learn to value our friends and their love for us. Taking them for granted is not the way to keep a relationship alive. Friends and friendships develop in due course of time. At times we connect with people instantly, but sometimes it can take months or years to develop, though once it is established it is a friendship for life.

Try not to let misunderstandings hamper your relationship. Communicate with your friends as much as you can and do not let external forces poison your feelings for them. If you trust your friends, trust them wholeheartedly. Do not let negative thoughts come between the two of you.

At any step if we falter it is perhaps the greatest blessing to have a friend to support us. True friendships are hard to find and true friends even more difficult. So if you come across any, keep them close to your heart and do not lose them over petty issues. Work hard towards preserving this bond. A friend lost is a life lost. Try not losing any!

Know Thy Neighbour!

We make our friends; we make our enemies; but God makes our next door neighbour.
—Gilbert K. Chesterton

Ok let's face it, we all need neighbours!
Who is the president of America? Of course you know the answer.

Who was the winner of this year's IPL? Well, of course, you know it.

Okay, so now let me ask you, what is the name of your neighbour?

And damn, here comes the dampener! I know that you might be aware of what goes on in the world and might be familiar with the minutest details of an international celebrity's latest scandal, but when it comes to knowing the name of your next door neighbour, you are clueless. This is the reality almost everywhere.

The bitter truth is that we have no neighbours in our lives. What type of world do we live in where the concept of neighbourliness is on the verge of extinction? ? Is this good or wise?

The more you think about it the clearer the answers will be. Good neighbourly relationships are not just advisable but are essential and practical.

People with greater IQs know it. Intelligent and smart people will agree to it.

And any thinking person will recommend it.

After all, a neighbour is next to one's kin.

Think of an emergency. Who is the first to arrive? Not your brother or sister or best friend, as they stay far away, so naturally it is your neighbour.

Thus, is it not wise to be on friendly terms with your neighbours and treat them as family?

Yes, of course it is.

Unfortunately, in today's fast paced life very few people have the time to get to know their neighbours. Despite living nearby we hardly interact with them or share life's little moments. It is easier to ignore them or be at odds with them, rather than on friendly terms because that requires effort and time and these are qualities that are in short supply.

I, like many others, have grown up on stories about neighbours being an integral part of one's life. Not just families next door but the entire locality or mohalla, as it was called, shared such strong bonds that it was almost like living with one large happy family. It's hard to find such examples these days. In fact, the present generation takes the meaning of the word 'neighbour' in a very literal sense and treat them as people living next door and nothing else. How sad and unfortunate this is.

We know all too well that few people have time for the small things in life, but extending a hand of friendship to one's neighbours does not require much effort. Exchanging pleasantries, chatting with them, jogging or going for walks with them, wishing them on festivals, inviting them over for a cup of coffee or a meal, these are very small gestures that go a long way in cementing friendly bonds with the people who live next door. We need to stop being arrogant and selfish and realize that having good neighbours is always beneficial. If your relationship is strong, you can always depend upon your neighbour in times of emergency, like your child falling ill, a sudden mishap.

Having good neighbours makes life more secure and less complicated. We can rely on him for even small everyday things, like keeping an eye on your house in your absence and such forth. Neighbours do not demand special attention or time yet they are ready to help whenever they can. They are not like a distant cousin who will remember you when a favour is required.

What else can we ask for in life? And isn't an understanding and caring neighbour a godsend? Learn to be amicable with your neighbours, socialize with them as these gestures will only extend your circle of dependable and trustworthy people, if nothing more.

Different Shades of Love

The concept of love is exciting! Some love with great intensity, but cannot express it. Others love for years, but don't speak of it. And then there are those who declare love loud and clear before it even happens. Love can be expressed in different ways. But whatever the means of expression, it is the one single emotion that can make us experience life in all its extremities.

Love makes war and love makes peace.

Love makes a bumpkin a poet and can also destroy a brilliant mind.

Love creates hope and can also lead to depression.

Love makes you laugh and love makes you cry.

Love can lead to friendship as well as enmity.

Love inspires your mind and also sets it on fire.

Love makes your eyes sparkle and it also makes you blind.

People love in many ways and in many styles. One person may love his cricket bat more than any other possession while another cherishes his school bag. And yet another loves his bike, but will happily give to a friend he loves.

People love the living as well as the dead, the real as well as the imaginary, an object or a subject.

Love can happen at any age, at any time and with anyone, no matter what caste, creed or gender. If love creates barriers, it also has the power to break them. Love can be personal as well as universal. Some love the body, others the mind.

However, love can be dangerous too, when it becomes an obsession. Unrequited love can be a dark and destructive force and should be controlled because it goes against its concept of togetherness, respect and honour.

Love is such a strong emotion that it even has a month dedicated to it. In February we celebrate Valentine's Day, a day dedicated to St Valentine.

It is believed that Valentine was a third century priest in Rome, at a time when Roman Emperor Claudius II decided that only single men made better soldiers. He thus prohibited young men from marrying.

Valentine, realizing how unjust the decree was, continued to perform marriages in secret. When the emperor discovered this, he ordered that Valentine be put to death. While in jail, Valentine probably fell in love with his jailor's daughter, and just before his death, he is said to have written letters, signing off with 'From your Valentine', a phrase that lives on. And since that day, 14 February is celebrated as the day of love.

Many in India have condemned Valentine's Day as yet another example of Western influence on Indian culture and tradition. But what we fail to understand is why this day is celebrated. Instead of forcing the youth to suppress their emotions, we should encourage them to celebrate Valentine's Day decently and within limits.

Every February, processions are taken out and demonstrations held to prevent the youth from expressing their love. Often, these protests turn violent and unruly. How ironic can this be? That violence should mar a day dedicated to love.

My question is that even if this is a Western concept, how does it harm anyone's sensibilities? Love never hurts anyone, so why shouldn't a day that promotes it be welcomed with open arms? We live in a democratic country, thus each individual should be allowed the freedom to live life the way they want to. And if it is to spend a day with one's beloved, why should people object?

Love has many forms—that between parents and child, husband and wife, siblings, friends, lovers. However, Valentine

Day is associated with the love between a boy and girl, man and woman.

To the youth, I would like to say, celebrate this day in the right spirit and maintain its respect. By upholding its sanctity and spreading the message of love and peace you can silence the critics and agitators.

The world today is full of strife—war, corruption, rape, molestation, murder, theft—so what better antidote do we need than to spread the message of love and peace for all mankind.

If we really want to honour St Valentine, we should celebrate love in all forms. Surround yourself with your loved ones—grandparents, parents, spouses, siblings, lovers, colleagues, friends and others. Shower them with flowers, chocolates and other gifts. If you are taking your love for a date, consider donating food to the destitute, or gifts for the poor, disabled, aged. By supporting noble causes we can widen the scope of Valentine's Day and spread love to a larger audience.

Part 3

Be Positive

*Once you replace negative thoughts with positive ones,
you'll start having positive results.*

—*Willie Nelson*

Hope and light are positive elements. Remember this in times of loss and sorrow, when the future seems bleak and without hope.

Imagine a child who is brilliant, ambitious and who is looking forward to a good education. Suddenly, he loses his father, the only breadwinner in the family. Instead of a bright future, he will now have to step into his father's shoes and take responsibility for the family.

Imagine the plight of a young wife who loses her husband unexpectedly.

Think of a promising businessman who becomes bankrupt.

My friends, there are innumerable such cases which can shatter the security and dreams of a person.

What then is the solution?

Should we fall into deep depression and curse our circumstances?

Definitely not. There is no person, whether rich or poor, who does not experience the trails and tribulations that life confronts us with. It is how we cope with them that is the test of our endurance and spirit.

I believe that a positive attitude towards life is the greatest treasure. By being positive a person can fearlessly face any situation in life, no matter how terrible.

It is not so difficult to be positive.

Shutting out negative thoughts, accepting the present as a bad phase, looking ahead for a better time are just some of the ways to convert negatives into positives.

Remember, after darkness there is always light. There is no doubt that hope is a light that shines through the dark moments of our life. It is the greatest tonic that can help us overcome negative thoughts and actions.

In the face of adversity don't succumb to depression. Instead muster up courage and make a determined effort to work harder and get your life back on track.

Act positive, think positive. Be confident.

Create a whole new positive world around you. Throw out malice and negative thoughts and get inspired by the lives of famous men and women who persevered despite all odds. I would like to give some examples about people for whom hope was the guiding star in their journey through life.

Thomas Alva Edison: More hope, more light

It is a well-known fact that Thomas Alva Edison became deaf when he was twelve. Despite this setback, he revolutionized the world by inventing the electric bulb, phonograph and telegraph system. Such was his determination to prove to the world that physical disabilities can be overcome if there is a will.

Marla Runyan: the born blind

At the age of nine, Olympian runner Marla Runyan developed Stargardt's disease, which is a form of macular degeneration that left her legally blind. Runyan began to make her mark as a world-class runner in 1999 at the Pan American Games. The following year Runyan became the first legally blind person and paraolympian to compete in the Olympic Games in Sydney, Australia. Marla finished eighth in the 1,500 metre, the highest finish by an American woman in that event. In 2002, Marla finished as the top American, with the second-fastest debut time by a woman, in the New York City Marathon. Runyan also holds several American records for various running events.

She proved to the world that hope, positive thinking and will power can make the impossible, possible, and set an example so that others could draw inspiration from her achievements.

Louis Braille: the eyes of the blind

Braille went blind when he was just three years old. But his disability did not daunt him. Instead, his weakness proved to be his biggest strength. He invented Braille, a writing system that enabled the visually impaired to read and write, thus benefitting blind people throughout the world.

Sudha Chandran: hope has many legs

Sudha was born in Chennai and completed her masters in economics from Mumbai. On one of her trips back home she met with a terrible accident, which resulted in the amputation of her right leg. But this tragedy did not deter her. Using an artificial leg, she returned to dancing and is now one of the most accomplished proponents of Bharata Natyam and has received many awards.

Helen Adams Keller: hope blooms any time and in many ways

This legendary lady was the first deaf and blind person to become a Bachelor of Arts. It was her teacher, Annie Sullivan, who taught her how to communicate by spelling words with her hands, following which Keller became a prolific author. The two of them travelled extensively throughout the world, particularly Japan, where they had a huge following.

Keller actively campaigned for women's rights as well as other social causes. In 1920, she helped establish the American Civil Liberties Union (ACLU), a nonpartisan, nonprofit organization which defends and preserves individual rights and liberties.

President Franklin D. Roosevelt: Hope never dies

When Roosevelt was thirty-nine, he was afflicted by polio and became paralysed. Yet, his political life thrived and he went on from being the governor of New York State to the president of the United States, the only president to be elected four times.

And so my friends there are endless examples of people who have defied all odds to survive and succeed.

Yet, how many of us have considered the plight of the physically challenged and those with special needs? And of those who look after them? Most of them have a normal upbringing because their families believe that they deserve to live like others do. If this is not hope, what is it?

'Hope is light', 'hope is life'. Let this become our anthem in our endeavour to bring hope and light to those in need.

A positive attitude helps one greatly in getting over one's blues and prepares him to battle everything that life throws at him with determination.

One Pledge at a Time

Determination has tremendous generative power. It is full of immense possibilities. It refines our character on one hand, and expands our vision on the other. Those wanting to bring about a radical change in their lives must not hesitate about making new resolutions. Only a strong determination can help overcome procrastination.

A new year always brings hopes and dreams. It is also the time for fresh beginnings, a time to look at life retrospectively and promise ourselves a new beginning. Making new year resolutions is a common practice, some are followed through, while others die a sudden death.

What baffles me most is why can't we stick to our commitments? Why not surprise ourselves by simply fulfilling the resolutions we have made? And we certainly do not need to wait for the new year to achieve that.

A slight change in our attitude can make a difference. It can leave us happy and satisfied in the end, and ultimately make our lives more meaningful.

Just take one pledge and aim to fulfill it.

- I will not tell lies this year
- I will try to control my anger
- I will stop smoking
- I will spend more time with my family and friends
- This year, every month, I will donate a fixed amount to the poor

- This year, every week, I will help the destitute lying on the pavement
- This year I will save money so that I can buy blankets and food for the homeless
- This year I will educate at least one child from the slums
- This year, once a week, I will visit an old-age home
- I will not litter and help others develop a civic sense.
- This year, I will be more caring towards my parents
- This year, I will not bribe anyone to get things done
- This year, I will stop overspending and start saving
- This year I will be more responsible at work

Our greatest treasure is our determination. It ensures our happiness and success in life.

Thus, my friends, it is easy to make your own wish-list, but remember to stick to it. Strike off those that have been kept and then move on to the next.

Pop the Happiness Pill

For every minute you are angry you lose sixty seconds of happiness.
—Ralph Waldo Emerson

Unhappy people are as common today as they were in the past. Ask anyone you meet and the typical answer will be: 'I am not happy.' Could it be true that people are really that sad or could it be that happiness eludes us? Or is what we see or hear merely an illusion? It is entirely possible that those opulent houses are just a façade for the unhappy people who dwell in them. Or that a smiling face hides an unhappy heart. It has been a long time since I met a truly happy and contented person.

Does this mean that we are living in unhappy times? And, is there no way to achieve happiness? I don't think so.

Although a recent survey conducted by Ipsos, an international research company, ranked India as second among the happiest nations in the world, the reality is different. Rising prices, corruption, gender inequality, are just some of the acute problems we face, which gives rise to the question: 'Are the people of India happy?'

What is happening to my country and her people?

Every day a new problem arises, but the country continues to survive and function. We have either learned to live with such situations or to find a way out of them. We have not allowed the bad times to drag us into an abyss. Instead, we as a people have grown stronger and are now ready to face those hurdles. Perhaps it is our will to fight and survive that has given us a second place in the survey.

Discovering how to live happily is the key to contentment. There is no magic formula behind this, it is just to make the effort to do a good deed every day.

Freeing ourselves from worries and renouncing the joys of the materialistic world are some of the ways. Others could be listening to music, watching a dance recital, travelling, entertaining our family and friends, reading a book, relaxing, going to the gym or going for a jog. In fact, yoga and meditation are the best ways to cleanse your system.

If you want to be happy, get to know yourself because the answer lies within. Forget worrying about the future, for what we have today is what matters most to make us happy. Discard bad memories and whatever baggage you may be carrying, and go ahead and enjoy the moment.

There is no doubt that happiness is an attitude. A positive approach towards life ensures it.

Love life and make the most of it.

Blame the Blame-Game

An eye for an eye makes the whole world blind.
—*Mahatma Gandhi*

Let us be generous about the faults of our fellow human beings. A pretentious person is too intellectually blind to appreciate the qualities of other people, or to rise above petty issues and consider the larger picture. However, it is time to prove to your country that you are a responsible citizen and that you care about her future.

I am good. You are bad!
It's not me. It's you.
It's not my fault. It is yours.
I am not telling a lie. You are!
I am not corrupt. You are!
I never argue. You do!
I am not bad, but you are.

Take a look at the blame game that is enacted in the political arena all the time. Whether inside or outside Parliament, our politicians are busy washing their dirty linen in public accusing each other of wrong doings. The BJP may be against the Congress on corruption issues and scams such as 2G, CWG, Adarash, Coalgate and others, but when it concerns the Yeddyurappas in their own party, they sing a different tune. And if their stand on that issue is questioned, it is seen as a political vendetta. This example aptly demonstrates the national attitude of saving oneself and accusing the other. This attitude has been universally adopted and is practised not only in politics, but also in every aspect of daily life. In all situations, no matter how big or small, there is always someone who will be playing the blame game, rather than attempting to right the wrong. Just because we think that we are free from flaws, does that make us God's equal? Does it mean that we as individuals can't and don't make mistakes or do any wrong? By continuously blaming others, are we not projecting a bad image of ourselves as well as the country on a global level?

We assume that it is permissible to find fault with others, but then we should be ready to accept our flaws and shortcomings. Anyone can put the blame on someone and walk away from the situation, but only a very few will take the responsibility to rectify matters. Would you not like to be among those few? Or are you happy to be part of the crowd? Rising above petty issues should be the aim. Mudslinging indicates a poor character, while accepting a mistake is an act of courage. You make the choice.

If you think deeply enough, you will realize that instead of developing a more positive, cooperative attitude, playing the blame game will only make us more negative and scheming. Wouldn't it be better if we could channelize this energy into trying to resolve issues rather than finding faults and picking fights? Being positive in mind, thought and deed symbolizes maturity and is also representative of a person's culture and background.

In order to project a picture of India as a progressive nation, we must adopt the 'forgive and forget' approach instead of showing our more vicious side. We, as citizens of India, must unite to contribute in whatever small way we can so that this dream will become a reality.

All our remedial measures for overcoming the inimical elements in life and society reveal the quality of our thinking. Lex talionis cannot be an ideal model for a civilized society.

Any blame game is retaliatory in character.

Prayer for Peace

Peace comes from within. Do not seek it without.
—*Buddha*

Peace is the highest form of attainment in the human life. In fact, the one who attains peace is the one who achieves everything in life....

Peace. How precious this word is. It is what everyone yearns and wishes for. Day in and day out, people struggle in their daily lives to find one moment of peace but all in vain. Is it really that hard to achieve? How come that in such a huge population very few can confidently say that they are at peace with themselves and with others? We can easily achieve peace by shunning our personal greed for materialistic values and power, then why has it eluded mankind for centuries?

Have you ever tried to discover the reason behind our restless nature? There is little time to sit and contemplate why this is so, but there is every possibility that the answer lies within us, yet we are unaware of. Is this an issue of the times we live in? Are we so busy that we cannot find a few moments to relax and focus on things that really matter? How ironic! We run around everyday trying to achieve more and more so that we can satisfy our ambitions, yet we find it hard to set aside a few moments for our own peace of mind.

In our search for peace, we practise yoga, meditation, spiritual experiences and other therapies, attend counselling sessions and such forth and yet we are dissatisfied. Distressed about this, we search for peace in materialistic goods like money, luxury cars, ostentanious homes, partying, clubbing and yet we are still unhappy.

If this is so, where exactly is peace? What is its real source and how can we achieve it? The answer probably lies elsewhere.

I think that we should not just aspire for peace, we must work hard each day to achieve it.

And that is only possible if we keep on practising it till we perfect it. The best way is to pray for it.

Most religions tell us that prayer is the only possible solution to any irremediable problem in life. A sincere prayer for peace is always answered.

My request to all of you is to make this an everyday habit. But don't be selfish in your prayers as you won't get the desired results. Praying that your loved ones, family, friends, neighbours, fellow countrymen and others to be equally blessed should make you content with life. Practising prayer in its purest form will certainly bring about a change in your outlook and open your mind to more positive thoughts. This will just be the beginning and from then on, you can continue to welcome more joyous and good thoughts through the power of prayer.

Mother Teresa: An Inspiration for Generations

The lotus is a flower that grows in muddy waters and yet its beauty is a feast for the eyes. We admire it because of how it makes us feel. Similarly, among people there are very few who inspire and encourage us to do something for the cause of humanity, not for their origins but for the impact they leave upon us. Mother Teresa is one such person. An inspiration, a god for a generation of those who have passed and those who are yet to come! She devoted her entire life to the cause of lepers and destitute children. The more she helped the closer she moved towards being accepted as a symbol of love, care and devotion.

At a time when a person ignored or avoided the underprivileged Mother Teresa was a godsend! Her life story does not follow the conventional path, yet it is an inspiration for every human being—her passion for the service of humanity was admirable and very rare.

She was born Agnes Gonxha Bojaxhiu in Skopje, Macedonia on 27 August 1910. Her father was a successful merchant, and as a result, she had a comfortable childhood. However, by the age of twelve, she realized that she wanted to become a missionary.

When she was eighteen, she left her home and entered an order of Irish nuns that ran missions in India. With some financial help from voluntary supporters, she started an open-air school for the homeless.

Later, she was given permission by the Vatican to start

her own order—Missionaries of Charity. 'Helping the helpless is the best way to get connected to God' was the sole maxim that motivated her far beyond the limits of her mission. Starting with only twelve members, the order now has more than 4,000 nuns, who have worked selflessly to better the lives of children in Latin America, Asia, North America and Africa. Mother Teresa's mission today has spread its roots deeply throughout the world.

She has helped people affected by floods, epidemics, famines and many more calamaties, shown them a better world. She has embraced them when they only knew hatred and tears. We must perpetuate her heritage.

We should all join hands and support causes which help the homeless or the underprivileged.

Make a start by working in groups and regularly visiting homes in your neighbourhood asking for old, discarded clothes. You can also ask them to donate food that has a long shelf life. In this way, no food will be wasted and will reach those who really need it.

Once, we think beyond our own selfish needs, we will discover an entirely new world within us. Happiness depends on our inculcating ethical values. A 'me-centric' attitude is definitely not the way for spiritual growth.

We need not become nuns or priests to aid the needy, all we need is the willingness to help.

So what are you waiting for? Every minute is precious. Go! Help all the people you can in any way possible. Remember that even the smallest of gestures can go a long way.

Peace within is the most potent elixir of life.

Positive is What Positive Does

Believe it is possible to solve your problem. Tremendous things happen to the believer. So believe the answer will come. It will.
—*Norman Vincent Peale*

There is always light at the end of the tunnel! In an earlier chapter, I had talked about the significance of a positive outlook. Now I am going to discuss how being positive in both mind and action can help negotiate the joys and sorrows of life.

It is often observed how failure or loss of hope can lead to depression and gloom, and in this state of mind many tend to fret and fume and take drastic life-altering decisions. The cycle of negativity that they get trapped in forces them to curse their destiny and move towards doom.

This negative attitude is paralysing, it even numbs a person's energy and vitality.

A bad or unexpected academic result, loss of a job, lack of timely promotion, a business crisis, break-up of a love affair or even the loss of a parent or loved one, can destroy one's, enthusiasm, vigour and zeal. It feels as if life has come to a standstill. Nothing seems right and the whole purpose of living seems meaningless. We lose our zest to lead a normal, positive life and the only solution seems to be ending it all.

It is estimated that over 100,000 people in India commit

Positive is What Positive Does • 133

suicide every year, that is more than 10 per cent of the number in the world. Sadly, this rate has been increasing steadily and has reached 11.2 (per 100,000 of population) in 2011 registering a 78 per cent increase over the value of 1980 (6.3). The majority of suicides occur among men and among younger age groups. Despite the gravity of the problem, information about the causes is insufficient.

It is sad to know that at times like these we often forget that life is not a bed of roses. God never promised us a happy and joyous life. We have simply assumed that life should conform to our terms and conditions whereby we can control our own happiness and sorrow. But we must realize that nothing is permanent and that life is always changing. We need to understand that if there is darkness today, there will also be light, and that what goes down has to come up.. We just need to cling on to hope and think about the positive aspects of life. After all, life is what you make of it.

The need is just to understand how life flows and to be positive. Such an attitude is certainly not an end in itself. It's a means to an end. Which means that while being positive in mind one must be positive in action as well.

And that pays.

Avoid negative thoughts and emotions at all costs. There should be no place for anger, doubt, hatred and greed as these are negative emotions. Instead, we should promote feelings of love, care, sharing and understanding, as these are the ones which will always keep us in a positive state of mind and the action that follows will surely bring good results.

Positivity comes from your actions too. If you are good to others, good will be done to you as well. One should try to do as many good deeds as possible in life, irrespective of what you get in return. God has his own way of rewarding you. Therefore, make it a point to treat your parents, brothers, sisters, friends and even strangers with love and compassion.

Make it a point to do some physical exercise, yoga or meditation each day will also keep your body and mind in a positive state and in high spirit.

Have faith in God and face problems or hard times with a cool and calm mind. Accept it as God's way of testing one's patience. Be who you really are and try not to fall into depression when times are hard. Remember that only those who work hard achieve something in life.

Take control of the situation. Do not allow the situation to take control of you.

I do understand all too well how difficult it is to be positive, even after trying so hard. You are perplexed and often baffled about what exactly to do. But do not lose heart my friend. It is at times like these that having a positive and happy atitude can help you overcome any barrier.

Destiny does play a major role in deciding which path our lives should take. In fact, our control over our lives and that of destiny go hand-in-hand. The influence of destiny is immense and drawing on examples from daily life will help elaborate on how fate can shape a positive mindset.

Instead of running to astrologers to find answers to life's problems, we should turn to God. Praying always cleanses our minds and thoughts of negative vibes and helps us develop a pure and positive outlook. Moreover, a stress free and clear mind always has the energy to revitalize life.

Although astrology is a science and there are several genuine astrologers who can guide us to move through life by taking few effective steps, but unfortunately, there are many fake ones as well, and I advise you not to get tempted or succumb to their designs.

Follow a few maxmins that will fill you with positive and happy ideas and thoughts. Be kind and donate to the needy. Help them to whatever extent you can.

Remember, charity for a genuine cause will always reward

you in much bigger and better ways.

By doing so you can win the good wishes and blessings from many happy people.

Take care of your parents. Love them and respect them.

Be nice to them and look after their needs.

Give food to the poor at least once a week.

Make it a habit to take care of animals and birds. Provide them with food, and water.

Such little deeds will go a long way in shaping your mind and life.

I am sure, however dark the future may look, light and life will soon embrace you with warmth.

My hope is that there will always be light in your life.

Thought for Food

A large number of people in this country do not have enough food to eat, yet there are many who throw lavish parties with huge quantities of food that often go waste. Is this not an alarming enough fact?

Every second child under three is malnourished and that too at a time when the India's economy is the fourth largest by purchasing power parity (PPP)!

These facts were hard to digest but easy to believe, especially since I have actually witnessed how food is wasted.

The other day I went to a posh restaurant, without realizing what the special buffet had in store for me--food for my stomach or food for thought! As we entered the restaurant, a waiter approached us to show us our seats. I was impressed with the quality of the service. When I looked through the menu, I was left dumbfounded. It seemed to me that there were hundreds of varieties of food to choose from—fifty kinds of salads and soups, an array of Asian, European, Continental, Mughlai, Mexican and other cuisines, varieties of imported fruits, hundreds of desserts—you name it and there it was on the menu.

Looking around I saw people enjoying their meals. But when I looked more closely I was confronted by a shocking reality. A reality that made me bow my head with shame at the thought of those BPL (Below Poverty Line) families for whom one square meal a day is a struggle. The amount of wastage I saw filled my heart with pain.

While millions in the country starved, here were people who

filled their plates, and just nibbled at the various dishes. They were not eating to fill their stomachs because they were hungry, it was more because they wanted to tickle their taste buds with what was on offer. Most likely, the food that was wasted was going to be thrown into the dustbin, and would not be sent to an old age home or orphanage or be distributed among the poor and homeless.

Suddenly a thought came upon me. The mountain of food that I saw at that restaurant could easily feed about 200 poor and destitute people at a time. Did the management not think about this fact or do such noble thoughts not strike people with wealth and the means? Why do they allow food to be wasted instead of distributing it among those in need?

But this restaurant is not the only culprit. It has become a common sight almost anywhere and everywhere we go. Thousands die because of the lack of nutrition or food, and yet large quantities of food go waste every day. Even though the government announces millions of tonnes of food packages for the poor and BPL families, we all know how much of these actually reach them and in what quantity.

It has been estimated that one in four of the world's malnourished children is in India, more even than in sub-Saharan Africa. Shocking, isn't it? For years the country has been debating about what to do about hunger and the poverty that underpins it, even though the food produce has increased. On paper there are millions of dollars of networks in place but too often, marred by corruption and mismanagement they tend to fail.

Now consider this.

As per Justice Wadhawa Committee and Arjun Gupta Committee and other reports, thirty-eight crore people earn a daily income of below Rs 20 in the country,

46 per cent children below three are underweight,

79 per cent are anaemic, 58 per cent of pregnant women

suffer from lack of nutrition.

The country's health problems are increasing rapidly. No wonder, the food problem is a grave one.

What a country we live in?

What type of mentality do we have?

What logic governs our lives?

Are we doing enough to fight this situation? Is it just the duty of government to think about these problems? As individuals, and most importantly as human beings, can we not contribute towards bringing an end to such problems? Of course, we can!

If we all share the responsibility and not leave everything for government to tackle, I am sure we can change the current situation. Besides, it does not take much effort to share our food with someone else.

If the World Bank and the World Hunger Index report carry this image of India then we have no reason to doubt the UN's report which estimates that 2.1 million Indian children die before celebrating their fifth birthday—four every minute—mostly from preventable illnesses such as diarrhoea, typhoid, malaria, measles and pneumonia.

I am yet to find an answer as to why a country as economically sound as India, where people have the means to buy the best of clothes, travel and enjoy good food, can still have such grave statistics. It is evident from the realities of malnutrition and hunger that India is a nation of extremes, where the poor keep getting poorer and the rich richer. While half the nation has the means and the money to buy anything they want, the other half is dying of starvation. And yet, India is still one of the fastest growing countries in terms of population and economy.

India's rating in child development rankings has fallen, putting it behind poorer countries such as neighbouring Bangladesh or the Democratic Republic of Congo, according to a new study by the Save the Children charity. Does this fact not humiliate us and make us ashamed? It is time for us now to think about the 'lesser blessed'. As the more privileged citizens, it is our responsibility to see that no child dies of hunger or malnutrition. Let every such death be a blot on our character.

We should learn to share our food with the needy and not cringe when they ask for something to eat. We should make it our duty to see to it that every malnourished child or woman we come into contact with gets at least one proper meal a day. This is the moment to think about the issues related to any form of wastage, particularly food. Let the entire nation learn the importance of frugality. Let each citizen understand the fact that by wasting food, we are depriving others of it. To solve such issues, we should not hesitate in taking stringent punitive measures. If new laws are needed then we should definitely make them.

The Golden Rule of Humility

Humility can take a person ahead of others. An adamant and arrogant person can never understand the essence of life.

We have the right to express our views the way we want to. This expression can never be curbed because this is how people, society and a nation mature.

But expressions must have humility and must respect another's sanctity. There should be limits on how freely we express ourselves.

But the question is who draws the line? Who decides when it is enough and how much is enough? Obviously it should be the person who is expressing himself. Unless this is so there will always be chaos in society. We live in a very sensitive world and, therefore, must avoid anything that can lead to social upheaval.

We need to learn lessons in humility. We must realize that by being humble we can build, sustain and strengthen relationships.

Unfortunately, it is observed that success makes most people lose their humility and sense of balance, and they become arrogant, whether it is a politician, bureaucrat, police officer or the rich and famous,

The powerful have little use of humility, they do not realize that by being humble they can actually bring people closer to them. Thus they can win more hearts than just votes.

It is important for all of us to be humble. Rash behaviour won't take you far nor will it help you win any friends. It will only complicate your life as well as others'.

History is full of examples of great people, who despite

reaching dizzying heights of success have not let their status rule their head--Lady Diana, Mother Teresa, the Dalai Lama, Ratan Tata, Sachin Tendulkar. Let people like them inspire you so that you too can learn to live life with humility.

Have Will to Succeed

Strength does not come from physical capacity. It comes from an indomitable will.

—*Mahatma Gandhi*

'I've had it!' is a phrase that has become a cliché today. It seems as if people neither have the patience nor the will to work hard towards achieving their goals. This upwardly mobile generation wants everything instantly. It is also true that modern technology keeps up with the fast pace of life. So to cater to this new age generation we have instant coffee, instant noodles, online payments, music and books that we can download and more. Whatever happened to the people who struggled so hard to reach a stage where they could enjoy these things. Does this mean that patience as a virtue is fast disappearing from our culture and time? Is today's generation so intolerant that they are ready to jump from one ambition to another in case they are unable to succeed in any within a given time-frame?

Yes, people have little tolerance today.

Have you ever wondered what would have happened if the greats like Abraham Lincoln, Mahatma Gandhi, Thomas Alva Edison, Willis Havilland Carrier or Louise Braille had given up their ambition midway because of the lack of will and patience? The world certainly would not have been the same. Even if these greats had faced great impediments, not once did they even think of giving up. They knew that the journeys they had embarked upon would be filled with obstacles, and at times failures, but for them it was more about the changes their work would bring and how future generations could benefit. Their patience was immense and their will was unshakeable.

Today's generation needs lessons in the virtues of will and patience. They need to know that a strong will can move mountains, that if it is your sole motivation in life it will bring you the success you deserve. Like us these greats were people who came from humble backgrounds, but what made them stand apart was their will to bring change for the betterment of mankind and society. We should, therefore, always tell ourselves that if they could do so, so can we. It is not necessary to be born in the corridors of power and wealth to be able to do things. One only needs the will to succeed.

Giving up on ambitions and aspirations is easy, but fighting to achieve it and working hard to attain one's goal, is stimulating. But today's generation is not entirely to be blamed. They live in an environment where everything gets done with just a flick of a finger. If they have to learn the importance of willpower they will have to step out of their comfort zones to experience life in all its realities. The need is to make them sit up and take notice of things around them.

Giving up one's ambition is not the solution to the problem. Besides, what value would ambition hold in your life if you are not required to struggle for it? Ambitions are not made overnight and definitely do not die in a day. Learn to value patience. It can help you achieve so much in life. Impatience can make people take wrong decisions in life only to regret them later. Be it the haste to get a job, marry, buy a house or anything. People often forget that in the long run any hasty decision can only lead to suffering. We all have one life so why live it with regret? Patience and a strong will have never made anyone suffer. On the contrary, it has only helped them achieve much more, as we have seen in the examples of greats.

Just like those great people, learn to be patient and persevere until you attain your aspirations and goals. Set realistic targets and chalk out a strategy to fulfill them. Never give up hope and always believe in yourself. Confidence in yourself can make you succeed beyond expectations. Never lose faith and always believe that God has a plan set aside for each one of us. Whatever is our due we will receive but in due course of time. Rushing things will only make us greedy and lose out on our real self.

So keep the will and momentum going!

Peace within is Life's Best Attainment

By enriching one's soul one can learn the secret of true tranquility.

In this world of great imbalances, mismanaged lifestyles, uncontrollable anger and growing frustrations, the first casualty is the quality of life, as most often there is little peace. Finding calmness and bliss has become a big problem, and all that we are left with are complicated lives, full of disturbing and sad experiences.

I have seen people living complex lives because of their insanely impractical attitudes. I have seen people's dreams, enthusiasm and zest for life falling apart like a pack of cards. I have heard many stories of woe around me, so much so that it makes me question if life really is that complicated, unhappy, disastrous and painful, or have we made it so because of our own shortcomings?

The fact of the matter is that we are living life the wrong way. Surrounded by many dreams and desires but with little discipline and dedication, we have successfully killed the wonderful spirit of life.

Take for example the rising instances of crime, deceit, infidelity, divorce, misunderstandings and mental health problems, as well as the cases of over-ambitious youth in a perpetual state of rage and you will find that the problem lies in our mistaken notions about how to live life.

It pains me to think of many bright and ambitious young people who lose their cool at the drop of a hat and take to indulging in unlawful activities.

Everyone wants to be rich and famous overnight.

And naturally everyone doesn't become one.

Everyone has a list of goals to attain—find a great job by twenty-two, buy a car and flat by twenty-five, and a few years later a bank balance of crores. After all life's enjoyments come only with money. Clubbing, pubbing, foreign vacation, parties are new age fundas that add glamour and glitz to life. Because of wealth and a free spirit many of our youth become the victims of the terrible cycle of disorderliness, violence and unsocial behaviour, or they just want to think big and dream big. Many of our high-spirited youth seem to be losing the battle of life because of wrong moves and over-ambitious want lists. They thus languish in the limbo of drugs or crime when none of their wishes are fulfilled.

It reminds me of the saying, 'if wishes were horses beggars would ride.'

Living a contented life is possible. But it only becomes possible when you learn to control your passions and follow the rule of working hard in a disciplined manner. Focus on the goal and steadily move ahead to achieve that on the basis of merit and confidence. That will reduce the unnecessary haste to achieve impractical dreams and the subsequent frustration and depression that follow.

Nothing happens overnight. One has to have patience and, most importantly, the will to plan your future.

There is great wisdom in sticking to your dreams and working systematically towards fulfilling them without taking shortcuts to success.

Keeping a calm and balanced mind will go a long way

in building up a more rational outlook with fortitude and equanimity. And that in turn will certainly reduce the levels of tension, stress and depression.

Lessons in Anger Management

Holding on to anger is like grasping a hot coal with the intent of throwing it at someone else; you are the one who gets burned.
—The Buddha

An angry mind is a recipe for stress, violent relationships and aggression. It will only bring you closer to destruction, alienate you from family, friends, lovers and disturb your equilibrium. Keep anger at bay if you want to have a positive and long life.

Constant multitasking, meeting deadlines and other demands of daily life are some of the pressures that make us angry. When things don't get done in the way we want them and as a reaction we begin shouting and screaming at others around us, we totally forget how our angry words have been hurting them. In a way we become insensitive to their feelings in those moments. And when we do, we feel embarrassed and try to find ways to mend fences. Why do we allow ourselves to get into such situations when we know that by being calm we can achieve something better?

Why do we fret and fume when confronted with situations that we disapprove? Is it because we are fast losing control over our lives?

Our lives, especially in cities, are becoming too demanding most of the time. Traffic jams, constant phone calls, EMIs to be paid, visits to the bank, the boss's demands, nagging relatives and friends are some of the irritants that make it difficult to maintain one's sanity. But is losing one's temper the answer? One must remain calm and not react to situations aggressively. Try not to become a slave to anger, instead enslave it to lead a stress-free and even life.

Research says that anger is the cause of many diseases—high blood pressure, hypertension and even heart attacks. Besides health problems, anger can lead to wrong decisions as well. Not only does it destroy the equilibrium, it also has a degenerative effect on our lives.

Kill anger, but not your health and balance of life. Anger management is not rocket science and does not require expensive aids or visits to a psychiatrist or psychologist. By taking a few easy steps we can make a huge difference to ourselves as well as to the people around us.

Why can't we do something to control anger?

Never lose your calm.

Always think twice before speaking. Whenever you feel angry, drink a glass of water or count from one to ten or do breathing exercise to help you relax.

Let pleasant thoughts or events fill your mind.

We shouldn't forget that human beings are prone to committing errors and that kindness and compassion are virtues of a great person.

Always speak in a pleasant manner. Try to talk sweetly as that would act as a great leveller to stop your anger and also of those who you are talking to.

Make it a habit to follow our great Indian values of humility, respect to seniors, love and care for all. Practise yoga and meditation as they never fail to harmonize the body and mind.

My young friends, if you follow these basic steps, you will notice a difference in your behaviour in just a week. The change will surprise not just you but also your family, friends and even strangers. More important, it will show you the benefits of leading a peaceful, stress-free life.

Do Good to Feel Good

When we perform a ritual, why do we observe every minute detail? Because detailing matters. If we make even the smallest mistake it can completely dilute the purpose behind the ritual and so we are extra cautious.

Forging relationships is like following rituals. If we falter along the way there is the danger of ruining the relationship forever. If we can take care not to do anything wrong while performing a puja or yagya why can we not be extra careful when handling a relationship?

Showing small gestures can build a lasting relationship and makes life more enjoyable and meaningful.

Just a smile, a hug, enquiring about someone's health or welfare, can go a long way in cementing the bond.

You can do that with everyone. Your wife, family, neighbour, friend, colleague, boss or even a stranger.

Just thank your wife for all the hard work she does to bring the family together and look after all their needs. It will definitely leave her happy and committed.

Be nice to your domestic help and staff, offering them few words of praise and encouragement. Or exchange pleasantries with your neighbours.

By gestures I do not only mean gifts; sometimes your behaviour and how you conduct yourself in public matters a lot. So try being cordial with everyone. If you are positive and happy you will infect your surroundings with the same feelings. Be warm in your interaction wth others. It will always leave a good impression on them.

Help an old or blind person cross the road.

Extend a helping hand to someone who has met with an accident. Provide them with immediate first aid or take them to a nearby medical facility. It may sound time consuming but your help can save a person's life. Gestures do not require much effort. They just require good intentions and will. Our culture and tradition has taught us to be good to others and help people as much as we can. Then why do we forget these teachings as we grow up? With time our intention to be good to people should intensify and not diminish. By being nice and caring for others we will gain good for ourselves.

It is time to refresh and renew our learning and rebuild a social bond.

I am sure ugly incidents of road rage, murders, accidents, rapes will disappear if we allow the qualities of compassion and friendliness to develop within us. It could be an end to many of the miseries we hear about.

Remember small gestures of love and friendship can bring about big changes in our life.

All good deeds generate positive forces.

Follow the Heart's Path to Invention

One good thing about young people is that they think big. Their dreams and aspirations are high and they prefer to build their lives around those goals. This attitude is certainly inspiring, but there is another side to this.

In their race to achieve their goals, their disconnect with the reality, results in the worst frustration and over powers the subject with all sorts of negativities.

The situation is very simple to understand.

Though most of our new age youth carry high aspirations and goals not all are fortunate to start their career in a right way.

For example, if thousands pass out from the IITs or IIMs or other renowned management schools or universities, only few get the opportunity to make it big from the start.

They are offered jobs at some top MNC or Fortune 500 Company, get paid lavishly and begin a career with a flourish. They fulfill their material goals almost immediately, which include a house, comfortable car, foreign vacations and such forth.

But the lucky ones are few and comprise about 10 per cent of the total number of young people who graduate every year.

What about others, the majority who are not so privileged? Even though they may have the same qualifications, dreams, ambitions, desires and wishes, they are hampered by lack of opportunities or luck. At times they don't have the right guidance and counselling on how to make the most of the opportunities they have. They start a career with a normal salary of say about 25,000 to 30,000 rupees a month and slog it out. For them big cars and bungalows seem a distant dream as they struggle hard to meet their daily needs. To them life is all about 9 am to 5 am jobs and then having to find more means of livelihood to livea comfortably every month. So this big gap between the few and the many becomes the bone of contention.

If he could get so much, why can't I?

If my friend can buy a car within few months of getting a job, why can't I?

If they can go for overseas vacations why can't I do the same with my family? Thoughts like these often occupy the minds of our youth and create a sense of discomfort, uneasiness and dissatisfaction.

This finally leads to anger, frustration and depression, when in spite of trying everything they cannot achieve what they desire.

It destroys the person's confidence and shatters his dreams. He starts to feel useless and frustrated and this in turn affects him personally and professionally.

So what is the solution?

The young should keep their feet firmly on the ground and open their eyes to reality.

There is nothing wrong in having big dreams, but one should always be aware of reality.

Remain steadfast to your goals, move ahead steadily and never lose balance. If the young explore other options, they will discover the immense opportunities before them. They just need to identify what exactly are they good at.

Many young people in the metros, and even smaller towns, have discovered many new business ventures based on their talents. It could be a bakery or bookshop, an interior design store or designer boutique, an art gallery, beauty parlour and spa. Today you can find stores selling antiques and jewellery, organic produce, accessories and much, much more. Such entreperauners not only mint money but they have also transformed their hobbies into enterprising business ideas. By using their talents they have taken the first step to achieve their dreams. More important, they enjoy what they do and are successful as well.

Such people are intelligent and creative, but just need an incentive to discover their latent talents. Earlier, professions like photography were taken up by selected few and were confined to photo studios. Now anyone who has a camera and some knowledge of angles can become a skilled photographer. Similarly, organic farming is now the latest fad. With people becoming more health conscious with each passing day, this enterprise cannot but succeed.

Besides, we live in an age where social networking sites are the tools used to connect people and spread the word about such business ventures. Such ventures do not take much investment.

Start small and spread the word around and soon you will have a huge network of followers and clients alike. One needs to expand one's vision and think of innovative methods and the world will be your oyster. There are so many avenues to explore and discover and the new age people are ready to embrace anything and everything that sounds interesting.

More than the money and materialistic gains every youth should aspire to develop ideas and thoughts that are different and dynamic. There is no dearth of talent in our country. The youth just need confidence and some guidance on how to proceed. If they are satisfied and happy pursuing what they really believe in, then all other benefits and luxuries will follow. Just let them follow their hearts.

Spiritual Dhongis

The world looks up to India for its spirituality and horders of soul searchers visit our country in the hope of attaining nirvana. They fervently search for godmen, sadhus, gurus and try to follow their path to find solace in life.

The same also happens to us Indians.

We have endless lists of babas, gurus, godmen, yogis, tantrics, sadhus and much more. Each of them have countless followers, who are godfearing people and are devoted to their gurus.

They depend upon their gurus to find solutions to their problems and consider them as the only solace and hope when troubled. As a result, these gurus exercise a great influence on the lives of their devotees. So much so that whenever they call, thousands of people come out in support of them. And this is what make a guru so powerful.

Here lies the real problem.

Following a guru for spiritual reasons is fine, but when it becomes political, it can create an unprecedented stir.

Today, democracy is all about numbers, and the opinions of the majority count. And so when a baba or guru takes up issues that go beyond spirituality, a large number of people support the cause without even thinking of the repercussions.

For example, when branded gurus and babas take up any issue, they gather huge crowds who follow them blindly without even knowing what their guru is advocating. The chaos that ensues because of such gatherings often leads to mismanagement in crowd control. By all means we are not criticizing them, but the point is that when we have so many political parties, activists, independent social workers and organizations to tackle these problems, why do men of spirituality jump into the bandwagon and endorse their point of view? Agreed it is a democratic country and every one has a right to voice their opinions, still wouldn't it be better if gurus and yogis and babas forgot their political ambitions and focused more on teaching lessons in religion and spirituality?

Many gurus also have a huge and very profitable business empires and huge bank accounts. They have schools across the country and even abroad, they organize overseas camps regularly, have properties outside the country. Some of them even have a direct or indirect link with the large business houses that are only driven on their vested interest. These connections amply corroborate the presence of rampant corruption.

Understanding the nature of politics in our country and all the games played in the name of democracy and citizen's rights, these gurus often fall into the hands of crafty politicians and uncouth businessmen to fulfil their secret ambitions. Imagine the kind of following these gurus have. If twenty of such gurus join hands for a cause, they can even overthrow a legitimate elected government just because of their money power and huge fan following.

Is this good for the nation?

Is this good for democracy?

Is this good for the smooth functioning of government?

Naturally, the answer is no. It is time, these gurus returned to doing what they do best—preach sermons on the benefits of attaining nirvana. They should stick to doing their jobs rather than dabbling in politics.

Dabbling in nonspiritual subjects creates more confusion and makes it difficult for most people to really know what these gurus want and what exactly is their role? It has been noticed that some spiritual masters talk a political language and even go to the extent of telling people which party to vote for. If this is so, they can always ask their devotees not to vote for the corrupt and criminals. But owing to their affiliation with some politicians, they encourage their followers to bring only those to power.

This has to stop!

I do hope our gurus with little knowledge of politics just do their spiritual job, which hopefully they understand better.

Let our gurus, godmen and babas play the role of spiritual leaders rather than political ones.

A Licence to Kill

Violence in any form reflects the steep decline in the moral values of a society. There is no doubt that excessive obsession with wealth is dangerous for human beings. Only a respect for law can restore society from falling into perpetual darkness.

Are we as humans becoming less tolerant? Is our anger taking precedence over everything else so much so that in a fit of rage we are ready to murder someone? Well, the recent spiralling cases of road rage seem to support the fact that our patience levels have gone down and that we are fast becoming victims of our own vanity.

With about an average of thirteen people dying every hour, India has topped the global list of road accidents way ahead of countries like China, the US and UK. The situation is grim as the numbers are only increasing. Stress, peer pressure, competitiveness, aggression and impatience, personal problems and economic upheavals are cited as major reasons for the often volcanic outbursts by people when they are driving. Add to this a heady mix of power and disregard for law and you have a sure shot recipe for disaster.

Wikipedia describes road rage as, 'aggressive or angry behaviour by a driver of an automobile or other motor vehicle. Such behaviour might include rude gestures, verbal insults, deliberately driving in an unsafe or threatening manner, or making threats'. The Global Status Report on Road Safety by WHO noted that most perpetrators fall between the age group of twenty-five and forty and come from influential and well-connected backgrounds. No wonder most get away with minor punishments or are given bail immediately. Does this mean that only the powerful and the influential have a right to live and can keep killing innocent people because they are confident that, at some point, the law and the judiciary will favour them? Does the life of a common man mean nothing? Are people of authority there to provide cover to the rich and beat the life out of ordinary citizens? These are questions for our judicial system to answer since time and again they have failed to live up to the expectations of the hoi polloi.

Every morning when you pick up the newspaper or switch on the television, you are bound to come across reports like 'Man shot by an unidentified person for brushing past his car' or 'A driver kills another for overtaking him from the wrong side. These incidents have become the norm not only in metros but even in small towns, and are so common that they are no longer shocking. Reading or hearing about them makes one wonder why do people resort to something as extreme as killing for a matter as trivial as overtaking or hitting a fellow driver's car by mistake?

This attitude is clearly reflected in the way people drive. Cases of road rage and aggressive driving are on the rise, not just here in India, but all over the world. If the traffic police are stricter with such offenders, accidents of greater magnitude can easily be avoided. It is important to introduce stringent laws for traffic violators so that they act as deterrents for those who think that they are above law and have the freedom to treat roads as their playground. Using rich and influential offenders as examples to set the system right will not be a bad idea either.

With the economy going downhill and the ever widening gap between classes getting deeper, people are losing their patience, which perhaps is one of the many reasons for inconsistent and aggressive behaviour behind wheels. Often, the situation can get completely out of control and people end up hitting and seriously injuring pedestrians, or as in few cases even killing them. The roads have become a battleground for the battered souls who have been let down by the evils of society. But is this really justified behaviour? Obviously no!

For every person killed in an incident of road rage or aggressive driving there is very little justice. Since it has been noted that 70 per cent of the victims belong to the lower income group, there is hardly any immediate monetary help available to their families. A mere compensation of a few lakh rupees does not last lifelong. The problem with our law is that a) it works at a snail's pace and takes years to reach a conclusion, b) it often favours the rich and influential, c) it has not meted out stringent punishment to the well-known figures who have been involved in such cases to set an example. Unless we hear of examples that belie the above three criteria, we will not see a change either in people's behaviour nor will there be a drop in road rage related cases.

The problem of road rage is a serious one. The careless behaviour of people is destroying the innards of society. Anyone can run down or kill someone without really bothering about the consequences. Since when have acts of killing and murder become the social norm? If the law doesn't bring these hooligans to task, who will? Is this the India we want our future generations to inherit? As citizens, don't we have the responsibility to restore the lost glory of our society and cleanse it of all its evils.

All incidents of road rage suggest a decline in human values.

Marriage of Souls or Status?

Marriages are made in heaven, but how well and industriously are they arranged and presented and controlled on earth by the humans! Indian weddings have always been talked about for their grandeur. The customs, festivities, ceremonies that form an intrinsic part of a 'big fat Indian wedding' is unlike any other wedding ceremony across the entire world.

The style of Indian marriage has gone through a sea of changes over the years. In early 1940s and 50s, the weddings were a quiet affair, and only required a nod of agreement between the two sets of parents without giving a choice to the girl and boy. Entire clans and communities used to pool their resources to make the main ceremony possible. A wedding in the area meant a wedding in one's own house and so everyone used to come together to help in the arrangements. There were barely any other functions apart from the main wedding and reception, which were accompanied by traditional wedding songs and dances. Family ties and the emotions attached with the occasion were given more importance than knowing who's wearing what. It used to be an intimate affair where the main concern was to ensure that the wedding went off smoothly.

The 1960s and 70s were the most colourful decades in Indian culture, thus there was a shift in the way marriages were solemnized and celebrated. Unlike the 1940s and 50s, when intermingling between the sexes in public was considered a taboo, the vibrant 60s came as a breath of fresh air. Influenced by the Flower Movement in the West, this free and liberated decade encouraged the youth to go out and have fun. Love was no longer a stigma and the notion of a love marriage became acceptable. Though the ceremonies still retained their old world charm, the events leading to the main ceremony became more elaborate.

The most drastic change in marriages was evident in the early 1990s. The boom in the Indian economy and globalization allowed Indians to explore the field of designer and readymade weddings. The ambition was more on the lines of 'if you have it, flaunt it', and with the birth of a wedding industry arrangements became more formal and structured. One just had to hire an event management company or a wedding planner and matters fell into place.

If you look at the trend today, most weddings look like events. The warmth that was present in the past has disappeared, and weddings have become more about displaying wealth, than bonding with relatives and friends. The most expensive champagne and exotic foods are served, and extravagant clothes and costly jewellery are worn. Events last for seven or eight days and each ceremony has a different theme, which also determines the venue. In a country like India, where the population is almost 1.2 billion, there are millions of millionaires besides thousands of billionaires, and a wedding is an occasion where they can flaunt their richness. There is no dearth of money among rich Indians today and their lavish weddings are a clear proof of this fact. Exotic flowers are flown in from Amsterdam and Bangkok for one single ceremony. Specialty chefs are called in from all parts of the world, and customized gifts are presented so that each and every guest goes home satisfied and happy. Indeed money is a major factor at such designer weddings. It goes without saying that smiles, hugs, 'jhappiya–phaphiya', all take place, but without any emotions from heart.

However, such wealthy weddings also have a positive effect on the Indian economy and community. Thousands of youth are employed in the wedding industry, whether in the event management company, the flower industry, the tent house and caterers who replaced the traditional halwais. There are also thousands of professional dancers who perform at weddings, and stewards who serve food and cocktails.

But the question is: is there really a need to reduce a pious and pure ceremony into a shameful circus of wealth display? Should money take the centre stage or should the bridal couple be given importance? Sadly, the weddings of the rich and mighty have been reduced to such sorry state where mindless media coverage, the paid attendance of political bigwigs and film stars and an unhealthy show of wealth have taken precedence.

It is tragic to see how one section of India is dying of hunger and poverty, while the other has enough to spend on various ceremonies. On the one hand, a poor farmer is forced to commit suicide when he cannot repay the loan of few thousand rupees that he has taken for his daughter's wedding, and on the other hand, there are those affluent people who have enough to pay politicians and movie stars to make an appearance at a wedding. It's a strange but a scary scenario. The thrills people resort to to gain attention are funny but what is even sorrier is how we are influenced by such stunts and try to re-enact them to suit our means. So if a billionaire like Laxmi Mittal had a designer wedding for his daughter, we too want at least one extravagant and costly function. Instead of sparing a thought for the poor and sharing a fraction of our wealth with them, we would rather have display of twenty different types of cuisines, which might even go waste as it's impossible for anyone to eat so many things at one go.

As people we need to understand that weddings should remain just what they are. Business alliances can be made inside conference rooms, but wedding venues are not suitable to crack such deals. As Indian citizens, is it not our responsibility to bridge the gap that is increasing everyday between the rich and the poor?

The least we can do is reduce our spending on such occasions and try to keep to the basics so that the other section of the country does not feel left out.

Any sort of showing off should be discouraged at marriages and other ceremonies by the conscious and rich members of the society. When the money saved from a splurge is spent for the happiness of the deprived ones, then it will be a source of greater happiness.

My Nature, My Mother

Forget not that the earth delights to feel your bare feet and the winds long to play with your hair.
—Khalil Gibran

Everything comes and everything goes.
Life is here, but life is not here.
Hope rises, hope crashes.
There is construction and there is destruction.
Man lives now, but man can die in the next moment.
Life can take drastic turns in a matter of a twinkling of an eye.
And in just any moment, anything can happen.

Nature can be capricious and unpredictable, and we never know what surprises she may spring upon us when we are least prepared.

For centuries, man has taken nature for granted. She has tolerated our greed, wants and desires as we have wantonly destroyed forests, the flora and fauna, without once considering the consequences of these actions. Our selfish needs have disturbed nature's delicate balance and harmony and now we are seeing the fury with which she strikes back—earthquakes, tsunamis, hurricanes and spewing volcanoes. The power of these disasters has made us acknowledge the mistakes we have made by denuding nature of her resources.

The catastrophic disaster in Japan has proved that no nation can escape the wrath of nature. It also proves how vulnerable mankind is, and how helpless. No matter what preventive steps or actions we may take, it is beyond our control to change the course of nature.

Nature has her own pattern. She will give you back exactly what you take from her. If you are kind and gentle, she will shower you with gifts in the form of a green, clean environment, lush landscapes, sweet fruit and beautiful, sweet-smelling flowers. She will provide you with grand vistas, idyllic and rejuvenating retreats and other benefits, and prove what a true friend she is.

There is no greater wealth than the wealth of nature. Mankind needs to understand this and stop amassing materialistic wealth by destroying the bounties she provides us with. We must stop this arbitrary destruction for our selfish needs.

Time has come for us to rectify our mistakes and pay for our faults. The revolt of nature has begun and if human greed continues, it won't be too long before mankind will have to face her fury again and again.

There are small things we can do to preserve our environment—stop deforestation, plant more trees, conserve green belts, discourage the use of plastic, preserve water, reduce your carbon footprint, work towards climate control and so on.

Just like Rome was not built in a day, these measures will not change the current situation overnight. It is a long and painstaking process that governments, institutions and other authorities must initiate and work towards to reap future benefits. As individuals it is our responsibility to stop this indiscriminate assault on nature, but to do this we first need to stop and think, to acknowledge our mistakes and to commit ourselves to living in harmony with nature.

An order or diktat can never be the motivating factor. Instead, each individual must be passionate about their commitment to nature and work towards conserving her bounty. We need to introspect, rethink, reassess our attitudes towards nature, and learn to live in harmony with her.

We need to put an end to the violations of our natural resources for our own survival.

Nature and its Pleasures

Daffodils

I wandered lonely as a cloud
That floats on high o'er vales and hills,
When all at once I saw a crowd,
A host, of golden daffodils;
Beside the lake, beneath the trees,
Fluttering and dancing in the breeze.

Continuous as the stars that shine
And twinkle on the milky way,
They stretched in never-ending line
Along the margin of a bay:
Ten thousand saw I at a glance,
Tossing their heads in sprightly dance.

The waves beside them danced; but they
Out-did the sparkling waves in glee:
A poet could not but be gay,
In such a jocund company:
I gazed—and gazed—but little thought
What wealth the show to me had brought:

For oft, when on my couch I lie
In vacant or in pensive mood,
They flash upon that inward eye
Which is the bliss of solitude;
And then my heart with pleasure fills,
And dances with the daffodils.

—William Wordsworth

Every morning we wake up to screaming headlines on scams, terrorism, rape, government apathy, disorder in Parliament, oppression, anticorruption protests, murder and mayhem. Surrounded as we are by such images and reports, we have forgotten that life is beautiful and full of natural delights and pleasures.

Spending time with Mother Nature, or thinking about her, are one of the things we have given up on. All we do is litter our vicinity. Ever thought of striking a relationship with the one that gives us so much and asks nothing in return?

When I say 'nature', I mean all the elements—the open sky, cool breezes, rain, sun, moon, rocks, trees, forests, flowers, birds, animals. Whether one enjoys a rainy day or watches a thunderstorm or takes a nap under a tree, the spectacle of nature is awesome. With so much to offer, one cannot stop marvelling at its wonders or its intricate designs. The shapes of leaves, the colours of flowers, the vastness of open sky, the warmth of sun, the beauty of moon...all these are natural gifts that we have received, and yet we remain oblivious to them. Why? Is it because we do not have time or because we have never really understood nature's beauty and positive effects?

It makes sense to allow yourself some time each day to interact with nature. In this way you can also spend time with your loved ones—a walk in the park, a picnic or a holiday by the sea or among forests or mountains. The beauty and majesty of nature can inspire you to such a degree that all petty arguments and resentments vanish. Instead, your mind is filled with positive and happy thoughts, and it is difficult to maintain your distance from loved ones.

Nature is meant to be enjoyed. It also acts as a natural stress-buster and spa, so why spend time and money to be pampered in closed spaces when you can enjoy a totally rejuvenating experience outside? There is no better soothing sounds than the pitter-patter of rain, roaring waterfalls or twittering birds. Watching the sun rise or set, flowers blossoming or leaves unfurling are some of the most beautiful sights.

So take a break and move closer to nature's pristine pleasures, rather than get stressed by mundane routines of life. Spending time with nature is a revelation, it will calm your mind and cleanse your thoughts of all negativity.

Once in a while, plan a holiday to the mountains or beaches.

The simple pleasures of nature make life so meaningful. One need not spend huge amounts of money to experience them, they are free and yet so full of quality. Take a deep breath and let the cool morning breeze caress you.

When you live life for yourself, many other pleasures evade you.

When you live a life for others, with others, life unfolds its beauty for you to enjoy.

In the same way, if you live with nature, she, with all her bounties, will touch you in every way, so that you can live a life that you often carve for but hardly experience.

Break free from the monotony of life and live a day with nature.

I am sure this will introduce you to the pleasures of enjoying life in many more ways than previously thought of.

A Cornucopia for All

The active reforms over the last two decades have changed India's landscape. Telecommunication, roads, grand airports, smart metro rails and booming real estate are some of the visible manifestations of India's growing prosperity. Some of the infrastructure growth has been almost spell-binding. But above all it is the rising power of the youth and urban middle-class that has been most exciting.

We now see a pulsating India, a transformed India, a new look India Change is everywhere—economy, markets, institutions, connectivity and even in our hopes and dreams.

What has made this possible is that while the world is growing older India is getting younger. Over 70 per cent of the population is below thirty-five and that makes India a young nation of a billion people, with a billion ambitions, a billion hopes, a billion sources of positive energy.

A number of our cities have been transformed just within a decade. India's infrastructure now boasts of some of the longest bridges, tallest buildings, world's largest solar power project, greater market complexes, high class entertainment centres, new educational institutions, multi-speciality hospitals, roads connecting villages and towns, better infrastructure for farmers, mobile phones in almost every hand. This new world also offers us infinite possibilities.

But there's a seamier side to this. The fact is that most of the benefits of the new growth era have mostly benefitted those who were already powerful and privileged. This lopsided growth can have extremely dangerous consequences.

If we fail to take remedial action to correct these anomalies, there is a distinct possibility of chaos taking over. But we need to continue to believe that good things will happen and India will achieve its dream of becoming a superpower. The youth will make this possible. The day is not for away when a vibrant India will be an object of wonderment for the whole world!

Epilogue

To some people an epilogue suggests the end of something. To me it means the beginning of things to come. Epilogues are never about the cessation of activities, it is about finding means to start new ones. Through this book I have tried to put that cycle of 'read–think–act' in motion. What you read here were not just words, but thoughts, ideas and real-life experiences. Random thoughts can never have a conclusion. Every day they take on new forms, new expressions and new sensibilities. They make a person a creator and precursor of what can happen as opposed to what should happen.

Therefore, while an epilogue suggests an end, it initiates a beginning too.

I hope these ideas will encourage you to put your thoughts to good use, I wish to thank my readers for their patience. Those wanting to comprehend life in totality must keenly study the significance of each of the events, views and examples shared in this book. In the hope to embark on a follow-up of these thoughts, I shall very soon be ready to connect with you once again.

Acknowledgements

Thoughts are thoughts. They could be ideas, feelings, dreams, directions, visions, missions or simple desires and more. Thoughts must not be locked inside. Instead, they should be allowed to speak and communicate!

I would like to thank Ashok Chaudhary for helping me put this book together. His creative inputs have been very inspiring and made me a better writer.

My deep and sincere thanks to the duo who did more than I could ever have expected: my son Sarthak and my niece Upasna.

Sarthak is a MS in chemical engineering from Carneige Mellon University, Pittsburgh. Despite his busy schedule, Sarthak would still spare time to discuss issues with me, provide me with new age insights and encourage me to complete this book.

And for my niece, I have much love, appreciation and admiration for all that she has done for me. Taking out printouts, editing, correcting, and above all, reassuring me over and over again that my concern and care for my friends, society, nation and humanity must be communicated to everyone.

I am equally thankful to my wife Rashmi Jain, my brother Rakesh Jain and my sister-in-law Promila Jain for encouraging me.

Made in the USA
Monee, IL
03 May 2026

49438686R00111